THE ROOTS OF UNBELIEF

By

James D. Bales, B.A., M.A., Ph.D.

Editor, *The Thinking Christian*

"*How can ye believe,* who receive glory one of another, and the glory that cometh from the only God ye seek not?"—Jesus Christ (John 5:44)

Published by

THE OLD PATHS BOOK CLUB

DEDICATION

To George S. Benson: President of Harding College.
Nationally known lecturer. Devout Christian.

INTRODUCTION

Not only without, but also within, Christendom there is wide spread unbelief in the Bible. In many pulpits things are said about the Bible which one hundred years ago were said only by professed infidels. Why is this true? What causes have operated to produce the widespread unbelief of our generation? What is it that is blocking the development of faith in their hearts and minds?

These questions the author has endeavored to answer in this book, which is the first of a proposed series on Christian Evidence. The author has not endeavored to say everything that could be said with reference to each of the causes of unbelief. Enough, it is believed, has been said concerning each of them to enable the reader to see that these causes are not really such as either must or in any way should necessiate the conclusion that the Christian faith is not tenable. But until these causes are dealt with it will be impossible for a person to believe in the Lord Jesus Christ. All the evidence in the world cannot make a deep impression on a mind in which certain ideas block a fair consideration of the evidence. This is well illustrated by the statement made to Huxley by one of his friends in reply to Huxley's question as to why, if the evidence for God's existence was so clear that he, Huxley, did not perceive it. " 'May I speak frankly?' asked his friend. "Certainly,' answered Huxley. 'It is because you are color-blind.' Huxley was silent for a moment, and then replied: 'And of course if I am colour-blind, I should not be aware of it.'"[1] There are many who are colour-blind and know not the real cause of their belief. They imagine that the fault is with the evidences of Christianity, when in reality the fault is with them and the attitude in which they approach the study of the credentials of Christ. To assist the sincere unbeliever in his search for truth this book has been written to help him see the attitudes and ideas which now blind him to the light of the gospel.

---

[1]Quoted by George Steven, *The Psychology of the Christian Soul*, London: Hodder and Stoughton, footnote, p. 272.

TABLE OF CONTENTS

CHAPTER I

THE MADNESS IS IN THEIR METHOD

Of some it has been said that they have method in their madness, but of others it must be maintained that their madness is in their method. The absurd, irrational, conclusions that unbelievers have come to, with reference to Christianity, are the results of the mental attitude which they bring to the study of the faith, and the method by which they endeavor to evaluate it. They may deny either, or both, the existence of God and the deity of Christ because they are unable to establish them by certain methods. They overlook the fact, which should be obvious, that a method which applies in one field may not apply in another. *The nature of the field which is under investigation determines the kind of approach which one must use in order to arrive at correct conclusions within that field.* When one tries to prove something by a method which is entirely unsuited to the establishment of a particular truth, he will fail. But his failure does not mean that the truth does not exist; it proves that his method is not fitted to the particular field and can only result in fallacious conclusions. He has made the mistake of demanding proof by means of a method unsuited to that field. He has demanded that the method settle something with which it cannot even deal. He is as mistaken as the man who maintains that fear, hate, love, feelings, ideas, and ideals cannot exist because he has been unable to discover them by means of the X-ray machine.

I. THE DETERMINISM OF METHOD

The above considerations make it evident that there is such a thing as determinism of method, i. e. that the method that one uses may rule out certain aspects of reality and make certain that only failure can result from the effort to evaluate, or even to discover these aspects of reality by that particular method. It is impossible for fear and love to be discovered by X-ray. It is impossible that a man can pick up ideas with forceps, put them in a bottle, shake them well, and end up with a system of philosophy from such a combination of thoughts. And the man who tries to do it in that manner is not casting doubt on the existence of ideas, but rather does he cause doubt as to his sanity. It is not a reflection on ideas, but on him.

This determinism of method has been recognized by thinkers in fields remote from the study of Christianity. V. J. McGill lamented, in "Some Queries Concerning Moore's Method," that in some cases important problems in psychological research are ignored for no other reason than the fact that they cannot be dealt with by some particular technique or method which an investigator has perfected. Some very important problems have been ruled out of court by certain investigators because they do not lend themselves to certain experimental techniques and statistical devices.[1]

Dr. Robert E. D. Clark, a scientist of Cambridge, England, has pointed out that "many people who have no first hand acquaintance with science, speak as though the method of determinism was so completely vindicated that there could be little doubt that it ought to be accepted as an article of faith for the whole of Nature. Such a view, however, has little to commend it. Every scientific worker comes across very large numbers of phenomena, and he mentions few which do not fit in with his theories. They are usually huge numbers of isolated observations for which no explanations are forth-coming, and unless they are repeatable they are forgotten. Science is only concerned with repeatable observations, and by its very nature, anything 'miraculous' is therefore out of its domain. The method of determinism could not be applied to a miracle, while on the other hand no one could expect a miracle to be repeatable when the *physical* conditions were made the same.

"The assumption of determinism is then a part of the method of attack used by science. But whether determinism is ever true as a fact is another question. Its success as a method suggests that a large part of Nature is determined, and this seems to the writer the most reasonable view to hold.

"Thus by reason of its nature, science automatically limits itself and is incapable of discovering whether determinism is uni-

---

[1]*The Philosophy of G. E. Moore,* p. 484. See also R. S. Lynd's statement on p. 484, footnote.

versal, or even whether it exists at all for certain. On the other hand the experience of free will indicated that the decisions we reach are not forced upon us from without. It is, therefore, very unnecessary to interpret our minds in terms of that which our minds have discovered (or think they have discovered) in the outer world. In other words our minds begin by dividing up the universe into two sections—the obective physical world and the subjects observing it. Between these there is apparently a great difference, but a study is made of those parts of the objective section which best fit in with determinism, and it is then claimed that determinism must apply to both sections of the world. The procedure is in fact a complete vicious circle. By using its own free will the mind decides what to think about, and after a few stages of reasoning concludes that it has no free will."[2]

This determinism is the result of strict adherence to *one* method which has yielded fruitful results when applied to the objective physical world and from which sweeping conclusions have been drawn concerning the subjective realm of mind, of thoughts, feelings, ideas, and principles. The vast difference between the *life* of an intelligent being, man, is forgotten when men make large, unjustifiable, leaps from the life-less, non-intelligent matter and its relationships to life and mind. With two realms in the universe—the lower as manifested in matter and the higher as manifested in conscious, intelligent man—these men interpret all of the universe in terms of the lower. This is because of their blind adherence to a method which they have found productive in dealing with matter.

William James, one of the most famous and beloved figures in the history of Psychology, pointed out this same danger of making an unwarranted extension of a method. When engaged in research in psychology he adopted the deterministic view for scientific purposes. This viewpoint, however, was met with the counterclaim of ethics, when one considered larger areas of life than those embraced in those psychological problems, which one investigated by means of determinism which was adopted as

---

[2]*Conscious and Unconscious Sin,* London: Williams and Norgate Ltd., 28 Little Russel St., 1934. pp. 54-56.

merely provisional and methodological. He regarded the claim of ethics as sufficient to regard the will as free.[3]

II. THE MISAPPLICATION OF A THEORY OF PROBABILITY

What would you think of an individual if he maintained that a proposition or principle in mathematics demolished the claims of Jesus Christ and demonstrated that He was a false prophet? Doubtless you would think that he was beside himself in trying to weigh the credentials of Christ by an appeal to some principle in mathematics. And you would be right. And yet, some do it. They "reason" as follows: Christians admit that there has been a multitude of false prophets and Messiahs. If, for example, out of one hundred who might claim to be the Messiah the Christians admit that all of them but one are making a false claim, it is hardly likely that the one is any different from the others, they reason. Thus the odds are ninety-nine to one that the hundredth is false also. The theory of probability, they thus argue, is against the position that Christ is right.

This same approach is made by some as they argue against the resurrection of Jesus Christ. "You will admit," they say "that of all of the billions who have died that Christ is the only one for whom you made the claim that He was raised to die no more." "Yes," we answer, "although the Bible tells us of some who were raised from the dead, yet Christ is the only one who had been raised *to die no more*." "Well," they reply, "since you admit that billions have not been raised the odds are overwhelmingly against Christ's resurrection."

To a type of mind which hears only *sound,* and does not look for the *sense,* this may sound like good logic, and establish the improbability of the resurrection of Jesus Christ. So to them it will likely come as a shock that this reasoning is fallacious and that it no more shows Christ false and the resurrection a fake or a misunderstanding than it shows that Franklin D. Roosevelt never lived and was never President of the United States.

---

[3]William James, *Psychology: Briefer Course,* New York: Henry Holt and Company, 1907, pp. 461-462. The entire quotation should be read by those who have access to James' work.

The error resides in the misapplication of the theory of probability which tries to settle the discussion concerning the Messiahship of Jesus, and His resurrection, on a basis which is entirely foreign to the type of basis and approach which is necessitated by the nature of the claims of Christ and the evidence that He was raised from the dead.

The theory of probability may be excellent in dealing with some things, but it is entirely out of place when used to settled matters which by their nature demand a different approach and a different type of examination. We shall illustrate this in fields in which the absurdity of such a mathematical approach is seen at first glance, and then in fields similar to that in which the claims and credentials of Christ are to be tested. What would you think of a friend who reacted as follows when you, who are an expert on music, told him that a certain piece of music had an excellent rating? Immediately he gets his scales and his footrule in order to weigh and measure that music to see whether or not your evaluation was correct? What would you think of the person who denied the beauty of a song simply because he could not measure it in terms of square feet? What about the man who declares that there is no power or beauty in a certain poem because he has been unable to take the square root of the poem? You would think—well never mind what you would think; but to say the least, it would not lead you to evaluate highly his approach to these things. However, these individuals are no more in error in their approaches to these different things than is the unbeliever who approaches the credentials of Christ in the manner which we have described.

To take illustrations more in the field in which one of the types of the credentials of Christ must be weighed, we turn to the field of history. Nero, a Roman Emperor, ruled for a period of time in the first century. Anyone who knows much about history, and the historical method, knows that Nero did live and that it can be established by the historical method. What would we think of the individual who reasoned as follows: of all the men who have ruled others, the historians admit that there was only one Nero who ruled at this time and place. Since in all the rulers both before and after him they admit that they cannot find another, the overwhelming probability is that they have never found a Nero. For certainly that which cannot be found among thousands and thousands of rulers is not to be found at all. If we had a friend who reasoned in that manner we would think either that he was jesting or that he was long overdue for a mental examination. On such logic we could prove that an individual does not exist. The individual would admit that in the billions who came before and the billions who may come afterwards that there was not and that there will not be another one just like him: that he is unique, unprecedented and unrepeatable. If out of the billions of babies born both before and after his birth not one of them was he, the odds are billions to one that he was never born. Surely, that which did not happen in billions of times would hardly happen at all, the theory of probability is against it. One more illustration and we draw the principle out of these illustrations and apply it to Christ. Would you consider it sound logic if a man argues that because thousands and thousands of roads do not lead to Chicago, that therefore the probability is that no road leads to Chicago? No, you would not consider this reasoning sufficiently sound to make you change your mind about a proposed trip to Chicago. It can be proved that there are such roads.

Historical events are unique in their nature. Once an event has taken place, or an individual has lived and died, *that* event or *that* person can not be demonstrated to have taken place and existed by any theory of probability. That particular event cannot be repeated. Even in laboratory experiments although one can perform an experiment similar to that performed by another person some years before, yet the performances of the experiment today do not prove that some other person performed a similar experiment at a certain place and time. With reference to such experimentation one could prove that it *could* have been performed but that does not prove that such a person actually performed it. Things like that must be established by testimony. And the existence of each person stands on its own evidence and its own evidence is not disturbed in the least just because there were billions of other people who were not that particular person.

Whether or not Jesus Christ is the Messiah, and whether or not He actually rose from the dead, will have to be determined by whether or not the evidence sustains His claims and the claims made for His resurrection. The truthfulness of His claims are not undermined because there are others who have falsely made claims. Counterfeits do not disprove the existence of the genuine article, and if the evidence concerning any individual bill is that it is genuine it is still genuine although a million may not be genuine. Those claims of Christ which can be tested by the historical method must be tested by that method if they are to be actually tested at all; to attempt to test mathematically those which give themselves only to the historical treatment is to have madness in one's method.

The fact that there are many who have claimed to be sent from God, and that many of them contradict one another, does not in any wise prove that they are all false. It does prove that they cannot possibly all be right. Conflicting stories might be told about an individual or an event, but that does not mean that there is no truth concerning those things, and that the truth cannot be established. What would you think of a judge "if there came several witnesses before him, and their testimony was opposite to one another, he would without further examination reject them all at once, and make their opposition to one another to be alone a proof that they were all false, and none of them to be depended upon." No, it is "reasonable, when testimonies are opposite, to weigh and compare those testimonies, in order to form a proper judgment concerning them . . . A just and impartial judge will not immediately reject the testimonies on both sides without examination, because they contradict one another, which is the method" which some unbelievers follow with reference to religion, "but will carefully compare them, that he may find out on which side the truth lies, and which of the testimonies is most to be credited, and will give his judgement accordingly."[4]

---

[4] John Leland, A *View of the Principal Deistical Writer*, pp. 255-256.

Once an individual has examined the credentials of Christ and has become convinced that Jesus Christ is what He claimed to be, does one have to continue and examine the claims of all others who have claimed to be the Messiah? Not at all. Of course, one is willing to examine their claims and show that they cannot be maintained, but when one has established that Jesus is the Messiah and that He thus speaks with authority, He becomes the standard by which others are measured and found false, for they contradict Him and fall far below Him.

III. THE ARGUMENT TURNED AGAINST THE SKEPTICS

The theory of probability used by the skeptic to discredit the miracles and events of the Bible can not only be thus shown to be misused, but it can also be turned against him. Our own experience cannot be applied to miracles, for our own personal experience is limited to those objects and events which come under our notice. So from our experience we cannot draw testimony against them, nor from the experience of any other individuals who did not witness them or investigate them where they took place and in connection with the people or things on which the Bible claims that they were wrought. The fact is that "there is testimony for them, and *none* against them. Many persons testified that they saw them happen, and none testify that they were upon the spot, and examined all the circumstances, and saw that they did not happen. As to the testimony of those who were not there, however *uniform* it might be, it does not bear at all on the subject. The *principles of calculation,* therefore, are more in support of miracles than against them."[5]

Thus, to use the weapon of our foe on him, since there are many that testify that they took place, and none has left testimony that they were there and know by personal experience that they did not take place, the overwhelming probability is that they did take place. If, for example, five witness that these mira-cles did take place, and none witnesses that they did not, the odds

---

[5]Mr. Somerville, quoted by Cyrus R. Edmounds, in an introduction to John Leland's A *View of the Principal Deistical Writers,* London: T. Tegg and Son, 1837, p. xxvii.

are five to nothing that they did take place. We do not, of course, use the number of professed witnesses to the miracles as the chief proof of the miracles; but rather the character of the witnesses; the nature of their testimony; etc. We are simply showing here, even on the skeptic's own use of this type of theory of probability, that his own weapon cannot only be turned aside, but turned back into the vitals of his own arguments.

The theory of probability can also be turned against the unbeliever by showing that the overwhelming odds are against the idea of chance as the creator of the universe and man. A vast multitude of things had to be just right or else the universe and life would have been impossible. If any one of them had been off balance life could not exist.[6]

All these considerations support the conclusion that methods exclude some things, as well as include certain things. The nature of the method determines what can be isolated and studied by means of the method. The failure to recognize this has been one of the fundamental failures on the part of some unbelievers in dealing with the evidence of Christianity. They have been unable to get the right answers because their methods have excluded these answers from the very beginning. It is clear, therefore, that an investigator of the credentials of Christ should ask, before beginning his examination, whether or not the method of investigation which he intends to use is suited to dealing with the evidence on which the claims of Christ rest.

Our attention shall now turn to the way in which the conduct of professed Christians has, in some cases, helped to create a bias against Christianity. This bias has led some to conclude that one whose life is bad cannot have the right creed. As shall be proved, one should ask whether or not the person is really living by the faith which he professes with his mouth.

---

[6]A. Cressy Morrison, a scientist, has clearly presented this fact in *Man Does Not Stand Alone*. This book is published by Fleming H. Revell Company, New York. Dr. Arthur I. Brown's book, *God's Masterpiece—Man's Body* (Fundamental Truth Publishers, Findlay, Ohio) shows that the body is too amazing a thing to be the product of chance.

Chapter II

THE CONDUCT OF PROFESSED CHRISTIANS
AS A CAUSE OF UNBELIEF

The conduct of some professed Christians has been a stumbling block in the path of some unbelievers. It is a justification, through rationalization, of their failure to believe. "An elder founded our Infidel Club," a young man in England replied to the question concerning the founder of their club. "We all know what a humbug he is, and yet he is one of the big religious men in town." They refused to have anything to do with Christianity because the elder's life had discredited it in their minds. There are others who call to one's attention the crimes which have been done in the name of Christianity. The Inquisition, they say, is a sample of what Christianity does when it gains the upper hand. Others point to the division among Christians and claim that the Bible cannot be true for it supports such conflicting doctrines as are advocated by various religious bodies; all of which claim that the Bible teaches their doctrines. Others identify, and thus reject, Christianity with the superstition of professed Christians in the mediaeval period. "Mrs. Humphry Ward has traced her departure from the orthodox fold to the studies of Spanish ecclesiastical history in which she was engaged on behalf of Dr. Wace's *Dictionary of Christian Biography*, and in the course of which her mind was shocked by the discovery of the superstitions and legends which had grown up in the Mediaeval Church.[1]

The criticisms will now be considered to see whether they are fair criticisms of *Christianity*, or whether unbelievers have failed to distinguish between Christianity and perversions of it, or lack of it. If these things are not a part of Christianity then no informed critic will identify them with Christianity and criticize Christian-

---

[1] R. E. Welsh, *In Relief of Doubt*, London: H. R. Alleson, 1903, p. 29.

ity on the basis of that identification. Neither would an informed critic, in such a case, justify himself by making such charges against Christianity: nor would he permit these perversions of Christianity to hide from his view or keep him back from an earnest consideration of the evidences for Christianity.

IT WAS CERTAIN THAT CHRISTIANITY WOULD BE CORRUPTED

"The best of things in this world are liable to be perverted and abused. Good is often made to assume the shape of evil, and then to be evil spoken of. Christianity is the very last system that could be anticipated to escape corruptions. Its doctrinal truths are so elevating in their character, and humbling to the pride of the human intellect, that man would be sure to distort their simple grandeur, and bring them down to the level of their own enfeebled perceptions. Its morality is so strict and pure,—being a discerner of the thoughts and intents of the hearts, and, admitting of no compromise with aught that is unholy,—as to induce those who are unwilling to follow its dictates, and yet anxious to have its sanction, to bend it to their own prevailing inclinations. Its rites are so few, simple, and destitute of attractions to the carnal mind, as to make it no matter of surprise that men who seek righteousness in mere outward observances, should add to their number, and render them meet for the lust of the eye. Christianity has been frequently so much corrupted in its doctrines, morals, and institutions, as to have rendered it somewhat difficult to trace any resemblance between the blotched copy and the fair original."[2]

OTHER THINGS HAVE BEEN CORRUPTED

"Every system of truth has been more or less corrupted under human influence. The sublime science of astronomy has appeared in the somewhat ridiculous shape of astrology. The simple science of chemistry, in the hands of the alchemists, was a science of sheer extravagancies. Natural philosophy was once represented by magic. Jurisprudence, rightly understood and applied, protects the helpless, shields the innocent, and promotes the liberty and prosperity

---

[2]Thomas Pearson, *Infidelity; Its Aspects, Causes, and Agencies,* London: Partridge, Oakey, and Co., 1854, p. 209.

of a state; but it has often been systematized into an engine of
lawless oppression. If these earthly things, which are by no means
uncongenial to human nature, or to variance with its predominat-
ing tendencies, have been corrupted in the hands of men, it is not
wonderful that heavenly things, in coming down to the earth,
should have been subjected to a similar influence. It might rather
have been anticipated, that, in proportion as the revelation from
above was purer and loftier than the principles of human conduct,
would men endeavor to distort and corrupt it.

"It is divinely promised that Christianity should never be
destroyed, but there is no promise that it shall, in every case, be
kept free from corruptions. So far from this, that, even under the
watchful presidency of inspired men, there were false teachers
who crept into the church and endeavored to pervert the Gospel
of Christ . . . the most influential and extensively spread form
of corrupt Christianity that ever existed, was clearly foretold in
the apostolical writings. They speak of damnable heresies, of a
falling away, of the man of sin being revealed and of the working
of the mystery of iniquity. Christianity is not, however, to be
confounded with its corruptions, or made responsible for them."[3]

I. THE SUPERSTITION OF SOME
PROFESSED CHRISTIANS

It is true that the "Mediaeval Church," as well as the modern
Roman Catholic Church, and certain other groups, had a great
deal of superstition. And yet, one who can read the New Testament and compare its teaching with that of these churches
knows that these superstitions are one thing and the teaching of
the New Testament is another entirely different thing. Faith is
not blind credulity or vain superstition. These things flourish only
as people get away from the Bible, as did the Mediaeval Church.
As men return to the Bible they drop these superstitions as is
evidenced by what happened when men during the Reformation
started back to the Bible they began to drop superstitions.

Christianity calls on men to prove all things and to hold fast
to that which is good. (1 Thess. 5:21). They are cautioned against

---

[3]*Ibid.*, pp. x 209-210.

FROM

Old Paths Book Club

5646 ROCKHILL ROAD

KANSAS CITY 4, MISSOURI

believing everyone who professes to be a prophet of God; instead they are to try those who profess to be of God (1 John 4: 1-2; Rev. 2:2). Paul told Christians to "Beware lest any man spoil you through philosophy and vain deceit, after the tradition of men, after the rudiments of the world, and not after Christ." (Col. 2:8). "Wherefore if ye be dead with Christ from the rudiments of the world, why, as though living in the world, are ye subject to ordinances, (touch not; taste not; handle not; which all are to perish with the using;) after the commandments and doctrines of men? Which things have indeed a show of wisdom in will-worship, and humility, and neglecting of the body; not in any honor to the satisfying of the flesh," (Col. 2:20-23). "Now the Spirit speaketh expressly, that in the latter times some shall depart from the faith, giving heed to seducing spirits, and doctrines of devils; speaking lies in hypocrisy; having their conscience seared with a hot iron; forbidding to marry, and commanding to abstain from meats, which God hath created to be received with thanksgiving of them which believe and know the truth." (1 Tim. 4:1-4).

These passages recognized that superstitions would come and they warned Christians against the traditions of men; against the will-worship which has no higher origin than the mind of men. And those who will take the trouble, and certainly they should take the trouble before basing an argument against Christianity on it, to trace the superstitions of the Roman Catholic Church to their origin will find that they did not have their origin in the Bible. Can a fair, and informed, person condemn Christianity for something which had its origin not in a knowledge in the Bible but in a lack of such knowledge of and obedience to the Bible?

We shall present one example of the superstition of the Roman Catholic Church, and show how it is contrary to the Bible. She teaches that in the Lord's Supper the fruit of the vine and the bread become the literal blood and body of Christ. The superstition is without authority in God's word, as two considerations make evidence. First, if such change actually takes place it constitutes a physical miracle; and you will find in the New Testament that physical miracles were discernible by physical senses. The Roman Catholic Church, however, admits that neither blood nor flesh, in the Lord's Supper, can be discerned by the physical senses. Therefore, we conclude that no miracle has been wrought for they still have all the properties of the fruit of the vine and of bread. *Second*, after Jesus had called the cup his blood (Matt. 26: 27-28); He called it the fruit of the vine: "I say unto you, I will not drink henceforth of *this fruit of the vine,* until that day when I drink it new with you in my Father's Kingdom." So it was still the fruit of the vine even after He called it blood. This makes it evident that Jesus no more meant that it was His literal blood and body, than He meant that He was a vine when He said that I am the vine (John 15).

The Bible is also contrary to the superstitious practices which are bound up in spiritualism. God said to Israel: "When thou art come into the land which the Lord Thy God giveth thee, thou shalt not learn to do after the abominations of those nations. There shall not be found among you any one that maketh his son or his daughter to pass through the fire, or that useth divination, or an observer of times, or an enchanter, or a witch, or a charmer, or a consulter with familiar spirits, or a wizard, or a necromancer. For all that do these things are abomination unto the Lord; and because of these abominations the Lord thy God doth drive them out from before thee." (Deut. 18:9-12).

These considerations, combined with the *fact* that where the Bible is read and followed by the people superstition wanes and is driven away, make it evident that no fair investigator can charge Christianity with the superstitious practices of some professed be-lievers who have wandered from the Bible.

II. CRIMES COMMITTED IN THE NAME OF CHRISTIANITY

Christianity, some unbelievers maintain, has been responsible for religious wars and for the horrors of the Inquisition. Again they have overlooked what should be obvious, i. e. that all that peo-ple profess to do in the name of Christ is not necessarily actually done by His authority. Only that can be done in the name of Christ which has been sanctioned by Christ. These deeds of horrors were done in the time when Christianity was covered over with a garb of paganism. They can happen only after men have committed the sin of going astray from the world and the spirit of the New Testament.

Can any one seriously think that following Jesus Christ resulted in these crimes? How could such be inspired by Him who taught love for both friend and foe? "Ye have heard," He said, "that it hath been said, An eye for an eye, and a tooth for a tooth, but I say unto you, that ye resist not evil; but whosoever shall smite thee on thy right cheek, turn to him the other also. And if any man will sue thee at the law, and take away thy coat, let him have thy cloak also. And whosoever shall compel thee to go a mile, go with him twain. Give to him that asketh thee, and from him that would borrow of thee turn not thou away. Ye have heard that it hath been said, Thou shalt love thy neighbor, and hate thine enemy. But I say unto you, Love your enemies, bless them that curse you, do good to them that hate you, and pray for them which despitefully use you, and persecute you; that ye may be the children of your Father which is in Heaven; for he maketh his sun to rise on the evil and on the good, and sendeth rain on the just and the unjust. For if ye love them which love you, what reward have ye? Do not even the publicans the same? And if ye salute your brethren only, what do ye more than others? do not even the publicans so? Be ye therefore perfect, even as your Father which is in heaven is perfect." (Matt. 5:38-48). Do men really believe that following in the steps of that Master who spoke these things, led to the Inquisition and religious wars? The apostle Paul wrote in the same spirit of the Master and said: "Bless them which persecute you: bless, and curse not." "Recompense to no man evil for evil. Provide things honest in the sight of all men. If it be possible, as much as lieth in you, live peaceably with all men. Dearly beloved, avenge not yourselves, but rather give place unto wrath; for it is written, Vengeance is mine; I will repay, saith the Lord. Therefore if thine enemy hunger, feed him; if he thirst, give him drink; for in doing so thou shalt heap coals of fire on his head. Be not overcome of evil, but overcome evil with good." (Rom 12:14,17-21). No person of discernment could maintain for one minute that the Inquisition and religious wars are the fruits of which the above teaching is the root. Even the Roman Catholic Church, that practiced, and still justifies, the Inquisition, admits that the New Testament did not teach that heretics were to be treated in such a manner and that the church of the first three centuries did not practice the Inquisition.[4]

The death of Christ and of Stephen set forth the spirit of Christianity and not the death-dealing spirit of the Inquisition and religious wars. Jesus said, of His persecutors and slayers, "Father, forgive them; for they know not what they do." (Lk. 23; 24). As they stoned Stephen he prayed for them saying, "Lord lay not this sin to their charge. And when he had said this, he fell asleep." (Acts 8:60).

III. DIVISION AMONG PROFESSED BELIEVERS

That a lack of unity is a cause of unbelief, has been recognized by many professing Christians. Thomas Pearson wrote: "The world has, in these conflicting sects and divisions, a hold which it had not in the primitive age of Christianity; and, without as-signing to the unity of the church that efficiency as a cause which some (with a view of precluding a higher agency) have done (Gibbon), we cannot doubt that its visible unity, short though its continuance was, has a strong subordinate influence in recom-mending the Christian cause, any more than we can doubt that the return of peace and unity will be powerfully instrumental in the conversions of the latter day. 'Nothing,' says Lord Bacon, 'doth so much keep men out of the church, and drive men out of the church, as a breach of unity.' And, as Isaac Taylor remarks, 'if we could only bring to view the secret causes of that infidel-ity which, it is to be feared, prevails among the educated classes, this now named—the scandal arising from religious dissensions —would probably appear to be one of the most frequent and de-terminative.' "[5]

There is a division, of course, which is right. It is right that truth be separated from error and for holiness to be separated from unholinesss. This is right in order that the approved be made

---

[4]*The Catholic Encyclopedia*, Vol. VIII, p. 26.

[5]*Spiritual Christianity*, p. 149. Quoted in *Infidelity* by Pearson.

manifest and that the corrupt may not contaminate the good. As Paul wrote to the Corinthians: "there must be also heresies among you, that they which are approved may be made manifest among you." (1 Cor. 11:19). Paul told them also to withdraw from a brother who had become a fornicator, for "a little leaven leaveneth the whole lump." "Purge out therefore the old leaven" (1 Cor. 5:6-7).

But through a failure to understand the will of the Lord Jesus Christ there are people who maintain that the divided condition of the religious world is a good thing. There are others who maintain that it is not. Is there in this a contradiction, a contradiction originated and perpetuated by the Bible itself? Does it support these conflicting positions, and many other conflicting doctrines which some believers in the Bible hold? Not at all. The contradiction is not in the Bible but in the misunderstanding of the Bible by those who believe it. This is more of an argument against the truth of the Bible than against the truth of anything else which people misunderstand. The causes of religious division, however, are overlooked by those who maintain that the Bible cannot be the word of God, because they say, it teaches all of the conflicting doctrines which are held by the Bible believers.

The divisions and conflicting doctrines cannot be charged to the Bible; there are other things to which they are chargeable. Among the causes of division are such things as the violation of the fundamental rules of Bible study; an unscriptural loyalty to men which builds up a spirit of faction; the effort to be wise above what is written; the unwillingness to be bound by what the Bible says; the failure to cultivate the scriptural kind of long suffering and tolerance; the lack of love; the failure to study the Bible; and the setting up of authorities other than the Bible; these things, and not the Bible, are causes of division and contradictory doctrines.[6]

Jesus Christ recognized that division would hinder faith, and thus He taught His followers to be one. In His Prayer to the Father, He said: "Neither pray I for these alone, but for them

---

[6]We shall not enter here into an examination of these, and other, causes of division. Some of them have been dealt with in the author's book on *Soils and Seeds of Sectarianism,* to which the interested reader is referred.

also which shall believe on me through their word; that they all may be one; as thou, Father, art in me, and I in thee, that they also may be one in us: *that the world may believe that thou hast sent me.*" (John 17:20-21) Division has been both an active and a passive cause of unbelief. An active cause in that people have blamed division on the Bible and have considered the Bible as an uninspired book because they conclude that the Bible supports divisions and conflicting doctrines. It has been a passive cause of unbelief in that religious division has tied up men, materials and time, which could have been used to preach the gospel to those who have never yet had an opportunity to hear and believe. They do not believe because division keeps them from having an opportunity to believe.

Anyone who can read, or who can listen while someone else reads, can read the above statement from the lips of Jesus and recognize that the Bible teaches unity. It teaches a unity that people can see and be influenced by; for Jesus prayed for unity that the world might believe and they would have to be able to know about the unity before it could influence them to believe. The high ideal of that unity is expressed when Jesus likens what He prays for unto that unity which exists between Christ and God. How, in view of these facts, can one blame the Bible with the religious division which exists today? The lack of the knowledge and practice of the Bible, and not the Bible, has been responsible for the division. Let not unbelievers condemn Christianity for that which Christianity itself condemns.

1. One of the Ways in Which Division Has Fostered Unbelief

If one asks why it is that the public schools, especially the Universities and Colleges, often have an anti-Christian influence the answer must be sought in the history of education in America. When America was first settled schools were established by the religious groups which had founded the various settlements. For example, in New England the Puritans established schools to help provide, among other things, instruction so that the children would know how to read the Bible. Harvard was established in order to provide training which would enable the colonists to have educated ministers after the ministers, which came with them from England, were lying in the dust. All of the first Universities and Colleges were established by religious people.

As time went on, the State saw the need for public education. If education was to be public and state supported it had to be non-sectarian. Members of one denomination would not pay tax money to support schools in which members of other denominations taught their denominational doctrines to the students. There was no state religion so there could be no state school in which some particular denominational doctrine was instilled. And thus denominationalism was one of the things which has kept the Bible, and the teaching of the Bible, out of the public schools. And it still keeps it out. As George U. Wenner wrote, "Even if Protestants could agree on some ground, which is improbable, what kind of a conglomerate would that be which would be acceptable alike to Roman Catholics, Protestants, Jews and Agnostics? The thing is inconceivable.[7]

Of course, the inroad of the doctrine of evolution, and of materialism, through teachers who gradually took over the guidance of American Education; as well as the exclusion of the Bible; has resulted in the great increase in agnosticism and other forms of unbelief.

The American people who are religious, and they are still in the majority, should insist that since the Bible cannot be taught in the schools as such, that nothing that is anti-Christian should be taught. And yet, although one cannot teach the Bible there today it is permissible in most states to teach doctrines which undermine Christianity. Professors who admit that evolution had not been proved, are yet permitted to teach it as an established fact and to say or imply that all who do not accept it are ignorant or dishonest in rejecting evidence. To attack the Christian faith, or the institution of marriage, in many Universities, would not bring as great a reaction among the Professors as would an attack on evolution.

---

[7]*Religious Education and the Public School*, New York: American Tract Society, 1913, pp. 32-33.

With the attacks, sometimes direct and sometimes indirect, on the basis of Christian faith, and the exclusion of religious instruction it is no wonder that many of the American young people are subjected to a severe strain on their faith and at the very period that many of them are going through a reaction against authority and restraint which extends even to the authority of religion.[8]

IV. THE CORRUPTION IN THE LIVES OF SOME PROFESSED CHRISTIANS

The immorality of some nominal Christians, as contrasted with the good moral lives of some unbelievers, has caused some so to stumble that they reject the Christian faith without an adequate examination of it. They identify the faith with the lives of persons who misrepresent or betray the faith. Before clearly setting forth the fact that these people do misrepresent the faith, and that it is unfair to judge Christianity by them, let us see how that many of the moral unbelievers are indebted to Christianity for these high moral standards. Just as certain as some professed Christians live far *below* their creed, just so some sceptics live far *above* their creed.

1. THE UNBELIEVER LIVES ABOVE HIS CREED[9]

Concerning the morality of unbelievers, the first question one should ask himself is: *Was the character of the unbeliever shaped by his present world outlook?* Did scepticism give birth to his code of morality and his commendable course of conduct? One of the close friends of the author may be characterized as a man who has the head of an agnostic and the heart of an orthodox believer. He was brought up in a religious background and for awhile he followed in the footsteps of his father who was a preacher. He finally lost faith and although he intellectually gave up the Chris-

---

[8]Those who are interested in documented reading which shows the drift from religion to unbelief in the American schools, even in many religious schools, should read Dr. Wilbur Smith, *Therefore Stand*, Boston, Mass.: W. A. Wilde Company.

[9]R. E. Welsh, *In Relief of Doubt*, London: H. R. Allenson, 1903, p. 57. Some of the material on this point is drawn from his chapter on "Good Sceptics and Bad Christians."

tian faith he never gave up in his life the moral principles which had been woven into the fabric of his character by his faith. *The man of no faith is the child of centuries of faith.* Even those who were not brought up in a religious family have, in the majority of civilized countries, been brought up in a general environment which is religious. Certain principles of the Christian faith, as applied to morality, have found their way into the moral fiber of our social structure and thus have become a part of the code of conduct of the majority of people, unbelievers as well as believers, for most people conform to the general level of society.

There are numerous examples of the control that Christianity maintains over the moral life of individuals who have renounced it intellectually. In Thomas Carlyle's *Sartor Resartus* one of the reasons a character advanced as to why he had not committed suicide was the influence of Christianity. "From Suicide a certain aftershine (*Nachschein*) of Christianity withheld me."[10]

The "aftershine" influences many. Comte "the founder of Positivism studied and prized no book more than the *Imitatio Christi* (also George Eliot's chief companion); and his altruism is only a poorer name for Christian love."[11]

"One is reminded of the spies who brought back a bad report of the land of Canaan, while all the time they bore on their shoulders burdens of rich grapes plucked from its vines, belying their report. Good sceptics bear in their lives and homes the fruits of the Christian soil which they depreciate. Their personal and domestic virtues, when rightly viewed, are a tribute and testimony in no small measure to Christianity, which still girds them though they may not know it.

'You criticise the soil? It reared this tree—
This broad life and whatever fruit it bears.' "[12]

And thus their lives acknowledge the validity of the virtues of Christianity.

[10]New York: A. L. Burt, Publisher, p. 165.
[11]R. E. Welsh, *op. cit. p.* 61
[12]*Ibid.,* pp. 62-63.

Andrew Fuller well stated, concerning some moral deists of his day, "the Scriptures having diffused the light, they have insensibly imbibed it; and finding it to accord with reason, they flatter themselves that *their* reason has discovered it. 'After grazing,' as one expresses it, 'in the pastures of revelation, they boast of having grown fat by nature.' And it is the same with regard to their sobriety. So long as they reside among people whose ideas of right and wrong are formed by the morality of the gospel they must, unless they wish to be stigmatized as profligates, behave with some degree of decorum."[13]

These as Renan wrote, have been nourished by the moral sap of the old faith.

Russell Lowell, in his *Letters,* well wrote that "I fear that when we indulge ourselves with the amusement of going without a religion, we are not, perhaps, aware of how much we are sustained by an enormous mass of religious feeling and religious conviction, so that, whatever it may be safe for us to think, for us who have had great advantages, and have been brought up in such a way that a certain moral direction has been given to our character, I do not know what would become of the less favoured classes of mankind, if they undertook to play the same game." In spite of defects, any system of religion related to Christianity, is "infinitely preferable to any form of polite and polished scepticism, which gathers as its vortaries the degenerate sons of heroic ancestors, who, having been trained in a society and educated in schools, the foundations of which were laid by men of faith and piety, now turn and kick down the ladder by which they have climbed up, and persuade men to live without God and leave them to die without hope. These men, indulging themselves in the amusement of going without a religion, may be thankful that they live in lands where the Gospel they neglect has tamed the beastliness and ferocity of the men who, but for Christianity, might long ago have eaten their carcases like the South Sea Islanders, or cut off their heads and tanned their hides like the monsters of the French Revolution." When the sceptic "has found

---

[13]*The Complete Works of Andrew Fuller,* London: Henry G. Bohn, 1845, p. 23.

a place on this planet, ten miles square, where a decent man can live in decency, comfort, and security, supporting and educating his children unspoiled and unpolluted, a place where age is reverenced, infancy respected, womanhood honoured, and human life held in due regard,—when sceptics can find such a place, ten miles square, on this globe, where the Gospel of Christ has not gone and cleared the way and laid the foundations, and made decency and security possible, it will then be in order for the sceptical *literati* to move thither, and then ventilate their views. But so long as these men are very dependent on the religion which they discard for every privilege they enjoy, they may well hesitate a little before they seek to rob a Christian of his hope and humanity of its faith in that Saviour who alone has given to men that hope of eternal life which makes life tolerable and society possible, and robs death of its terrors and the grave of its gloom."

We do not make the mistake, of course, of assuming that where Christianity has not gone there are no moral principles. There are certain laws of moral life and some of these can be discerned by mankind through its own experience. As Paul pointed out those who were without the light of revelation were still not without the light of conscience for in their own hearts they were able to discern some of the laws of moral life (Rom. 2:13-15). Then, too, it is the contention of the Christian that from God's original revelation to man there has lingered at least fragments of those moral principles in the traditions of mankind. Nevertheless, it is still true that in countries in which the Bible exercises a great deal of influence, that sceptics generally derive their moral principles, insofar as they are commendable, from the influence of the Bible.

Those who point to good sceptics and to bad Christians have failed, in the second place, to recognize that *the true nature of scepticism and its influence on morality cannot be fully tested in the life of one individual or of one generation.* As pointed out the man of this generation who is a sceptic may have been at first a believer. To adequately test the moral fruits of unbelief one would have a generation which had been reared on unbelief, and whose environment unbelief had created. What if a person, after residing a few years in Africa, wrote home: "You affirm that the inhabitants of Central Africa are dark-skinned. I have lived here for years and am not black!" "No! but even you are tanned! Is it much more rational for a man to say, 'I live without Christ and without prayer, and yet I think I am not less moral that average Christians.' Perhaps so—though one would need to see to your spirit's core to determine what is happening under the crust of moral habit. But bring up your children on that principle. Let society at large, also, dispense with the spiritual supports of Christianity." Then after a few generations are passed, after you have a generation which has been brought up on the creed of unbelief, then and only then have you the true product of unbelief. Then, and only then, can many full fledged sceptics be found to compare with the true disciples of Christ. Even now, however, it is possible to find sceptics who live down to their creed, but the unbelievers generally do not want to put these individuals forward as representatives of unbelief. They pay unconscious tribute to Christianity in that they select sceptic who are as near like a true Christian, in morality, that they can find. This sceptic they often compare with a *bad* Christian.

There are professed believers who live immoral lives, this we recognized. But *we do not agree that these individuals are representative of the Christian faith; instead they misrepresent it.* One may point to such characters to prove that some professed Christians need to possess in their lives the principles of Christ, but he cannot fairly point to them as products of Christianity. Their very desire to appear, or to try to appear, Christian is a testimony that they recognize that there is value in Christianity. They are not real sons of God, any more so than those who commit crimes in the name of liberty are the the true sons of liberty. And although we cannot keep these folks from calling themselves Christians, we stoutly maintain that one must be Christian, and not merely be called by the name Christian.

It might be well to remind a certain type of unbeliever, those who are *determinists,* that according to their theory these immoral Christians are not really immoral. They cannot help being what they are for their conduct is determined by non-moral laws with which no freedom of will interferes. Furthermore, these individuals are a product of strict determinism, of which the unbelievers also are products. So why criticize these men who cannot do otherwise than they do, according to the determinist's theory. It is also well to point out to the relativist in morality that according to his theory these immoral Christians are not really immoral for all morality, on this theory, is in a state of flux. And they have as much right, on the unbeliever's own theory, to justify their pretense to live the Christian life, as the unbeliever has for his failure to pretend to live a Christian life.

The fact that unbelievers call these immoral Christians hypocrites indicates that they know that Christianity did not produce such a life. If they thought that it had they would call these people true Christians instead of hypocrite, which term means someone who is pretending to be what he is not. Thus they should not stumble and turn away from Christian faith because of the lives of some professing Christians. The fact that some unbelievers have recognized that these are not true Christians is made evident when some of them say that in attacking "Christianity" they do not intend to attack Christ. But if they are not attacking Christ they are not attacking true Christianity for Christianity, briefly put, is following the Lord Jesus Christ. And that is all that we defend; we do not defend the lives of mere professed Christians, or of even sincere Christians whenever they fall short of the standard of Christianity because of their weaknesses.

It will be helpful if the unbeliever will remember that the Lord Jesus denounced hypocrisy long before this generation of unbelievers saw the light of day. No more severe words, with reference to hypocrisy, have come from the lips of any person than those that came from the lips of Jesus in the twenty-third chapter of Matthew. Let the unbeliever read that chapter to see how far Christ is from recommending or tolerating hypocrisy. No one had pronounced the doom of "unchristian Christians" more emphatically than has the Bible. How, then, can one find in the lives of professed Christians a cause of unbelief? Their immorality does furnish cause for a lack of confidence in departures from the Christian life, but it calls for an application of Christianity and not for a renunciation of it. And how inconsistent are those who condemn Christians, who are Christians in word only, with moral standards which they have borrowed from the Christian faith, and yet renounce the faith itself and think that these immoral Christians are an argument against the faith.

The real test, then, is not found in the life of an unbeliever who lives above his creed, and a Christian who lives below his, but between two individuals who are the product of their respective creeds. In such a fair test men will not blame on Christianity that which had its origin in a lack of Christianity. In such a fair test the Christian will shine, for one of the potent arguments for the Christian faith is to be found in the fruit it bears with reference to character. As Daniel Webster said, one of the strongest arguments for the Christian faith was the godly life which his mother lived. Carlyle maintained that "as to the people I see, the best class of all are the religious people—It teaches me again that the best of this class is the best that one will find in any class whatsoever."[14] Yes, it is *the best by test,* and those who argue against the *Christian* life are arguing against the very incarnation of goodness, honesty, love, loyalty, gentleness, and all of the other virtues that make up the life that is truly good.

2. Unbelief As a Reaction to a Personal Grievance

There are cases where an unfortunate personal contact with a professed Christian has driven some into unbelief. Dr. Thouless (in the Pyschology of Religion, p. 82) told of a Sunday-school teacher who became an atheist after his fiancee eloped with another teacher. The resentment against the person is turned toward the belief which the individual holds.[15]

---

[14]Froude's *Carlyle's Life in London,* I:133.

[15]For other examples of men—such as Professor Haldane, and H. G. Wells, who revolted against Christianity for emotional, as well as other, reasons which were connected with their experiences with professed Christians see Dr. Robert E. D. Clark, *Scientific Rationalism and Christian Faith,* London: The Inter-Varsity Fellowship, 39 Bedford Square, W.C. 1, pp. 35-46.

3. An Unfair Suspicion of Religious Leaders

There is an attitude which leads some to say, when one presents the case for Christianity, that "naturally he would say that it is true since he makes his living by it;" or "since he is converted to it; he is a partisan who cannot be trusted with an unbiased judgment in these matters." Clement F. Rogers once had a man to shout at him, while lecturing in England, that he would never believe a man who wore a clergyman's collar.[16]

To such individuals we would say: "Just whom do you think should present the case for Christianity? Those who believe it or those who do not? In fact, who would present the case for Christianity, and maintain that it is established, unless he is a believer in it?" When put in this way they should be able to see the fallacy of asking for someone who does not believe—and supposedly has no prejudice in the matter, but surely such a man would have a bias against it—to present Christian evidence. Of course, the man who presents this evidence is a convert. He believes that it is true, otherwise he would not argue that it is true. So instead of suspecting him one should conclude that he is convinced that it is true; and that he therefore earnestly desires that others believe it for there is much at stake. The listener should then examine the case to see whether or not it is sustained. But let no man suspect Christianity just because it is advocated by those who accept it and spend their lives teaching it. For no one but a hypocrite would advocate something which he did not believe. Would the unbeliever think that we were reasonable if we met their arguments by saying: "Well, you fellows would naturally be expected to justify your course of conduct; and unless you can find an unbiased believer arguing for unbelief we shall not notice the arguments for all other advocates of unbelief—being unbelievers—are biased.

In a recent fine work of apologetics, Hammond noticed and answered the same tendency to discredit the advocates of Christianity. "A very common criticism of apologists, particularly of

---

[16]*The Case for Christianity*, New York: Harper and Brothers, 1928, pp. 261.

the theological apologists, is that they are 'special pleaders.' The illustration is taken from the Law Courts. A barrister or councel is supplied with a brief, and he does his best for his client. Most business men who have the misfortune to be involved in a trade dispute do their best to secure a 'special pleader' of this kind. They would feel very helpless if they had to present their argument before the court without this trained assistance. Yet somehow or other the term 'special pleader' is regarded as invidious. The implication here is like that to which we have referred already, in which the scientist is presented as a truth-seeker, and the poor theologian as a fanatical upholder of outworn conceptions. It is obvious, of course, that when a man is defending a belief which means much to him he is always in danger of manipulating evidence. This danger is not confined to theological beliefs. But, on the other hand, it is usually the interested man of this type who advances knowledge. Just because he is possessed of strong convictions he marshals his evidence in an orderly and convincing manner. It is not fair to assume that because his beliefs mean much to him he will become intentionally dishonest. If his mistakes in this direction are due solely to everzeal, there will be plenty of others to try out his conclusions whose competing beliefs will reduce the possible danger to a minimum. Also, the careful student is fully sensible of the danger of a retort of this kind, and proceeds with the more caution because he is aware that over-statement may prejudice even a good cause."[17]

In conclusion let us observe that although no informed individual who is fair can blame these departures from, or lacks of, Christianity on Christianity itself, it is yet the business of every Christian to try to see to it that his own faith and life is in harmony with the teaching of Christ. In this way one's life becomes an invitation to, and an argument for, the Christian faith and not a stumbling-block in the path of some who may be seeking for the way, the truth, and the life.

Let us now consider how some unbelievers miss the truth because they begin in the wrong place.

----

[17]T. C. Hammond, *Reasoning Faith*, p. 16.

CHAPTER III

BEGINNING IN THE WRONG PLACE

The full force of the evidences of Christianity is entirely missed by some investigators because they do not start in the right place. More than one error of this nature is evident in the approach of some unbelievers, and any one of them can, unless the person becomes aware of what he is doing, keep them from seeing the reasons for the faith. In this chapter we shall deal with the following errors: *First,* the considerations of the mysteries of Christianity without first weighing its evidence. *Second,* a consideration of the objections to faith without first considering the positive evidence for it. *Third,* the failure to deal properly with the things which present difficulties for the investigator. *Fourth,* the failure to emphasize and act on what one does believe. *Fifth,* the false impression that Christianity can be examined without serious *study.* *Sixth,* the failure to recognize when a thing is proved. Let us now consider the first error.

I. FIRST WEIGHT ITS ADVANTAGES, THEN ITS MYSTERIES

What would we think of the logic and the reasoning of the individual who, when confronted with the evidence of the destruction of Hiroshimo, replied: "I cannot accept the idea that one bomb did so much damage, for it is utterly incomprehensible to me how one bomb can do so much damage." Even the explanation of that which takes place in the explosion of an atomic bomb seems fantastic. Even though one may have explained to him *how* it is done, it is still a mystery as to *why* it is that way, why it can muster so much power. And yet, the inability of a layman, or even of a scientist, to understand all the things which are involved, in no wise mitigates against the fact that one bomb blasted Hiroshimo. The evidence all points to the fact that one bomb did it, and a failure to understand either how or why, does not in the least weaken the fact that it did. And the person is both illogical and unreasonable when he demands that all mysteries in connection with it be fully explained and grasped before he will accept the fact.

Is such lame logic and unreasonable reasoning transformed into commendable intellection when it is applied to the credentials of Christianity instead of to the destruction of Hiroshimo? All true reason answers, No! And yet, it is the very way in which some otherwise intelligent persons treat the evidence of Christianity. Christianity is often rejected because some of its teachings are mysterious, not in that we cannot understand that they are taught, but in that no one can explain why it should have been that way instead of some other way; for example, why the atonement should have been necessary.

Why should it be thought unreasonable because there are some mysteries in the Bible, some things which may not appear reasonable to some minds? After all, if Christianity is what it claims to be, the revelation of God in Christ, we should expect some things in that revelation which are not fathomable by human reason. What would be the value of a revelation from God which contained nothing except that which was discernible or produced by unaided human reasoning? If there are mysteries in the book of nature, if we cannot understand everything there, how should we expect to understand everything in connection with the revelation of God through His book the Bible? One famous British scientist, Sir J. Arthur Thomson said: "We understand the *how* of a few things, the *why* of nothing." As he once wrote: "Science as science never asks the question Why? That is to say, it never inquiries into the meaning, or significance, or purpose of this manifold Being, Becoming, and Having Been,"[1] which we see in the workings of life and nature. No man can explain why grass, when eaten and digested, can grow feathers on a goose and hair on a cow; or how a black cow can eat green grass and give white milk and yellow butter. The man who refuses to accept these facts because his finite mind cannot fully explain them or because there is mystery involved, is a man who refuses to be guided by the facts and who has such an inflated

---

[1]Michael Pupin, Editor, *Science and Religion* (New York: Charles Scribner's Sons, 1931), p. 24.

view of the powers of his own mind that he concludes that whatever he cannot fully understand and explain simply does not exist. Why cannot any reasonable person see that since mysteries exist in nature that one need not be surprised because they existed in revelation.

Not only would one expect mysteries in the revelation which tells us of God; of man's origin; duties; and destiny; but the Bible itself tells us that there are things in it which were not discovered and not proclaimed by unaided human reason. Paul wrote that "my speech and my preaching was not with enticing words of man's wisdom, but in demonstration of the Spirit and of power: that your faith should not stand in the wisdom of men, but in the power of God. How be it we speak wisdom among them that are perfect: yet not the wisdom of this world, nor of the princes of this world, that come to naught; but we speak the wisdom of God in a mystery, even the hidden wisdom, which God ordained before the world unto our glory: which none of the princes of this world know: for had they known it, they would not have crucified the Lord of glory. But it is written, Eye hath not seen, nor ear heard, neither have entered into the heart of man, the things which God hath prepared for them that love him. But God hath revealed them unto us by his Spirit; for the Spirit searcheth all things, yea, the deep things of God, For what man knoweth the things of a man, save the spirit of man which is in him? even so the things of God knoweth no man, but the Spirit of God. Now we have received, not the spirit of the world, but the Spirit which is of God; that we might know the things that are freely given to us of God." (1Cor. 2:4-12). As Peter said: "First of all you must understand this, that no prophecy ever came by the impulse of man, but men moved by the Holy Spirit spoke from God." (2 Pet.1:20-21. The Revised Standard Version). In such a revelation we could not expect otherwise than that there would be things which are beyond unaided human reason. To ask why God has done some things as He has done is just as impertinent in the Bible as it is in nature. Things are as God has seen fit to reveal them in His word (although in the world sin has made things otherwise than God

would have made them) and it is ours to study that which is
revealed to us and live in its light.

Then, too, both the Bible and experience testify that there
is sin in the lives of men and women. Thus it would be expected
that the reasonings of sinful men would often be contrary to the
revelation of God's will for sinful man. Since the Bible and experience both testify that sin has brought disharmony into life,
how could we expect perfect harmony between the Bible and
the reasoning of sinful man? Especially would this be true of
those individuals who have rejected the true revelation of God
because it refuses to allow them to give free reign to their carnal
passions. These individuals claim that Christianity is utterly unreasonable and then they give way to a manner of life which is
fantastically unreasonable; and the fallacies and dangers of which
have been demonstrated in millions of wrecked lives and in the
teaching of the Bible. Of such unreasonable individuals Paul
wrote a searching indictment. "For the wrath of God is revealed
from heaven against all ungodliness and unrighteousness of men,
who hold the truth in unrighteousness; because that which may
be known of God is manifest in them; for God hath showed it
unto them. For the invisible things of him from the creation
of the world are clearly seen, being understood by the things
that are made, even his eternal power and Godhead; so that they
are without excuse; because that, when they knew God, they
glorified him not as God, neither were thankful; but became vain
in their imaginations, and their foolish heart was darkened. Professing themselves to be wise, they became fools. And changed
the glory of the uncorruptible God into an image made like to
corruptible man, and to birds, and four-footed beasts, and creep-
ing things. Wherefore God also gave them up to uncleanness,
through the lusts of their own hearts, to dishonor their own
bodies between themselves: who changed the truth of God into
a lie, and worshipped and served the creature more than the
Creator, who is blessed forever. Amen. For this cause God gave
them up unto vile affections: for even their women did change
the natural use into that which is against nature: and likewise
also the men, leaving the natural use of the woman burned in

their lust one toward another, men with men working that which is unseemly, and receiving in themselves that recompense of their error which was meet. And even as they did not like to retain God in their knowledge, God gave them over to a reprobate mind, to do those things which are not convenient; being filled with all unrighteousness, fornication, wickedness, covetousness, maliciousness, full of envy, murder, debate, deceit, malignity; whisperers, backbiters, haters of God, despiteful, proud, boasters, inventors of evil things, disobedient to parents, without understanding, covenant-breakers, without natural affection, implacable, unmerciful: who, knowing the judgment of God, that they which commit such things are worthy of death, not only do the same, but have pleasure in them that do them." (Rom. 1:18-32). They are like the unreasonable men of whom Jude said, "these speak evil of those things which they know not: but what they know naturally, as brute beasts, in those things they corrupt themselves." (Jude 10). The fact that their way of life degrades man and reason, and the fact that the Bible elevates man and purifies reason, should strike reasonable men as one of the characteristics of the Bible which demonstrates that it ought to receive careful, and even hopeful, examination.

II. Evidences Before Objections

The positive evidence of Christianity is obscure to the minds of some because they fail to approach it directly. Instead, they spend most of their time dealing with the objections to the faith and approach its postive evidence only incidentally as they happen to be brought into contact with it in their search for objections. Thus they fail to see it either in its fullness or in a clear light unobscured by the mist of objections.

"In no other instance perhaps besides that of Religion, do men commit the very illogical mistake, of first canvassing all the objections against any particular system whose pretensions to truth they would examine, before they consider the direct arguments in its favor."[2] "But why, it may be asked, do they make such a mistake in *this* case? An answer, which I think would apply to a large proportion of such persons, is this: because a

---

[2] Dr. Hawkins, *Essay on Tradition*, p. 82.

man having been brought up in a Christian country, has lived perhaps among such as have been accustomed from their infancy to *take for granted* the truth of their religion, and even to regard an uninquiring assent as a mark of commendable *faith;* and hence he has probably never even thought of proposing to himself the question,—Why should I receive Christianity as a divine revela- tion? Christianity being nothing *new* to him, and *presumption* being in favor of it, while the burden of proof lies in its opponents he is not stimulated to seek reasons for believing it, till he finds it controverted. And when it *is* controverted,—when an opponent urges—How do you reconcile this, and that, and the other, with the idea of a divine revelation? These objections *strike* by their *novelty,* by their being opposed to what is generally received. He is thus excited to inquiry: which he sets about,—naturally enough, but very unwisely,—by seeking for answers to all objections: and fancies that unless they can all be satisfactorily solved, he ought not to receive the religion."[3] But, as we shall show in the section on the unbeliever's inability to recognize when the case for Christianity is established, it is not necessary to answer all objections before the truth of Christianity, or anything else that is true, is established and accepted.

What should men do, then, when Christianity, which they have long accepted, is controverted? Dr. Hawkins pointed out that "sensible men, really desirous of discovering the truth will perceive that reason directs them to examine first the argument in favor of that side of the question, where the first presumption of truth appears. And the presumption is manifestly in favor of that religious creed already adopted by the country—Their very earliest inquiry therefore must be into the direct arguments for the authority of that book on which their country rests its religion." Richard Whately commented as follows on this state- ment of Hawkins, "But reasonable as such a procedure is, there is, as I have said, a strong temptation, and one which should be carefully guarded against, to adopt the opposite course; to attend first to the objections which are brought against what is estab- lished, and which, for that very reason, rouse the mind from a state of apathy."

---

[3]Richard Whately, *Elements of Logic,* p. 428.

"When Christianity was first preached, the state of things was reversed. The presumption was against it as being a novelty. Seeing that all these things *cannot be spoken against,* ye ought to be *quiet,* (Acts 19:36) was a sentiment which favored an in-dolent acquiscence in the old pagan worship. The stimulus of novelty was all on the side of those who came to overthrow this, by a new religion. The first inquiry of any one who at all at-tended to the subject must have been not—'What are the ob-jections to Christianity?'—but, 'On what grounds do these men call on me to receive them as divine messengers?' And the same appears to be the case with the Polynesians among whom our Missionaries are laboring; they begin by inquiring, 'Why should we receive this religion?' and those of them accordingly who have embraced it, appear to be Christians on much more rational and deliberate conviction than many among *us,* even of those who, in general maturity of intellect and civilization, are advanced considerably beyond those Islanders."[4]

This should be sufficient to convince the unbeliever that he has not dealt, and cannot deal, fairly with the claims of Christ, and thus fairly with himself, as long as he views it simply from the standpoint of seeking, or asking for, answers to objections. Objections may be dealt with in their proper place, but in order for them to be considered in their true light, so that they will not be so magnified that they hide the proof of Christianity, one must seek first the positive evidence for Christianity. Do-ing this the unbeliever will find that as he passes from unbelief to faith, that many of the objections will fade away or other-wise lose the force which they appeared to have when magnified; that others are solved by the postive proof for Christianity; and that others, although they may not be completely answered, no longer have serious weight against the truth of Christianity.

It will be very profitable also for the believer to keep in mind the truth which has been presented in this section. When he is faced with objections to the faith let him see them in their proper place instead of considering them apart from the sound reasons which establish Christianity. If he fails to keep con-

---

[4]Richard Whately, *Elements of Logic,* p. 429.

scious of this proper approach he is apt to be overwhelmed by the objections because he ignores the solid ground on which he is already standing.

Let us help cure this cause of unbelief by insisting that men take the proper approach and view the objections to Christianity in the light of the arguments and evidences in the favor of Christianity.

III. How to Deal with the Difficulties

As we have already indicated, the attitude in which one deals with the difficulties will determine whether or not he will deal with them successfully. We take some suggestions from Torrey as to how these difficulties should be dealt with. First, deal with them honestly in that you do not try to dodge or deny that you have found a difficulty. Second, deal with them humbly, do not imagine that because you have not found a solution in a few moments there is no solution; that others have not found a solution; and that you cannot find it. Third, deal with them with determination. Do not give up for there is a solution somewhere if you look long and hard. If you do not find the answer you may at least discover that the difficulty does not discredit faith. Fourth, deal with them fearlessly; men saw them hundreds of years ago and the Bible still stands. It has stood test after test and we need no fear that it will now succumb to criticism. Fifth, deal with them in the light of the rest of the Bible. There is nothing which explains scripture like scripture, and the more one knows about the Scriptures the better equipped he is to deal with any particular part of the Scriptures.[5]

IV. Emphasize What You Believe

"The question which has to be settled by all who are passing through the mental conflict between faith and unbelief is, which shall I emphasize? It is a sore and weary battle. There

---

[5]Those who are interested in books on the subject of "difficulties" should see George W. DeHoff, *Alleged Contradictions in the Bible* (214 E. Main St., Murfreesboro, Tenn.); W. Arndt, *Does the Bible Contradict Itself*, and *Bible Difficulties* (St. Louis 18, Mo., Concordia Publishing House); and R. A. Torry, *Difficulties in the Bible* (Chicago: The Moody Press, 153 Institute Place).

is this which is believed, and there is that which is not believed. There is this which can be accepted, and that which is doubted. But which is to be emphasized? Jesus never asks any man to be untrue to his convictions or even to his doubts and scruples. He wants all men to be honest. He acts in this way with this earnest and honest man who came to Him hesitating because of doubt, yet coming to Him with his faith, in spite of his doubts, and He will act in the same way still (Mark 9:24). What He asks is that men should emphasize their faith; that they should not allow their doubts to rule them; that they should come to Him with the little faith they have, and obey Him as far as they believe in Him.

"That is the way of escape from unbelief. There comes a great enlightenment to the soul that obeys Jesus in anything. Experience is a great teacher. Faith conquers when it is trusted. Faith enlarges itself and strengthens itself when it is followed. Put the emphasis on what you believe. Form the habit—the mental habit—of following the light as you see it. That is the vital matter. This is the way of life and peace and rest, because it is the way of growing faith and vision." There are many who do not pay any attention to the rest of the Bible because the story of the flood or of Jonah and the whale loom so large in their minds that everything else is blotted out. But are these to be allowed to close their minds to the many other things in the Bible? "Because men will not believe that Balaam's ass spoke to him, are they not to believe that God is speaking to them through the lips of Jesus Christ His Son?" "Even if your faith in the revelation of God that is contained in this book is limited to one truth, lay the emphasis on that, act upon that. There is no other way to get help for your unbelief, no other way of gaining faith in more of its truth." Follow the truth which you do see and accept and emphasize it, and you will be in a better frame of mind to deal with the difficulties and to receive the explanations of these difficulties which you will finally find.

"Lastly, in your intercourse with others act upon the same principle. Emphasize in your conversation the thing which you believe. Give your faith the blessings of sunshine and air. You rarely help yourself by talking about the things you do not believe, unless you talk to someone who has more knowledge and wisdom and experience than you have yourself. I remember once in my far-off college days, talking to a student friend about our mutual doubts. He told me of his difficulties and I told him of mine. I can remember still the deepening darkness which crept over us as we talked. We did not help each other in the slightest degree, we only increased the burdens under which we both laboured. We should have talked to each other about the things in which we believed. We were not wise enough to help one another out of the difficulties that we felt. One of us should have quoted the wise words of Goethe when someone came to him and taked of his doubts. 'Tell me,' said he, 'of your beliefs; I have doubts enough of my own.'

"Let us also who are older have this mercy on the young, that we do not tell them of the difficulties which we feel and the problems which we cannot solve. Why should we lay the burden of our minds on them? Why should we anticipate the days when they may feel that burden for themselves? Why should we darken the outlook on life for young eyes, and chill young hearts with our cold unbeliefs? It is faith that saves, not unbelief, not doubt."[6]

This does not mean, of course, that the older person will lie to the younger person; but it does mean that when we are believers, but are yet wrestling with some difficulties which somewhat disturb us, but do not shake our faith, that we should not constantly pour these into young hearts which have problems of their own, problems with which we can help them. Grapple with and solve your problems, and when the time comes that he is faced with these problems you will be able to help him reason his way through, or believe his way through, to the solution. If, however, while you are in the midst of the effort to solve the problem, you dump that problem into his lap, his faith may not be as strong as yours and he may thus break under it.

---

[6]John Reid, *The Uplifting of Life*, pp. 36-40.

He does not yet have as many reasons for his faith as you do, and thus the burden may be too great for his weak faith.

This fault may be fallen into by a teacher or a preacher who has already faced and solved the difficulty, but who fails to present the solution when he presents the problem. For example, he may preach on the subject of Christian Evidence. In the beginning of his sermon he may list a number of objections which have been brought against the Christian faith, and then he may turn his attention to and thoroughly deal with one of them. The objections which he has listed have been put in simple sentences, briefly referred to, and thus may easily remain in the mind of the hearer, who is facing the problem of belief and unbelief. These other objections may weigh heavily on his mind although one of them is thoroughly answered. It is easier to remember the brief statement of several objections, than the intense investigation of one of them. These objections could have been met by the preacher also, if he had the time, but they linger in the mind of the listener and in some cases he may think on them and gradually build up a bias, or at least doubt, which is unfavorable to Christianity. In such cases the sermon on Christian Evidence has done more harm than good, to this person, because it raised many doubts and settled only one. The thing for the preacher to do is to mention only that point with which he is going to deal. Although the one who raises a number of objections, and answers only one, may state that the others can be answered, he forgets that the listener may not have the knowledge to do it and that it may therefore bother him.

> "Talk faith. The world is better off without
> Your uttered ignorance, or morbid doubt.
> If you have faith in God, or man, or self,
> Say so; if not, push back upon the shelf
> Of silence all your thoughts, till faith shall come:
> No one will grieve because your lips are dumb."
>
> Miss Willcox, "Speech"

Doubts need to be faced, and talked over with those who can help us, but let us in ordinary conversation emphasize the reasons for our faith, and not our doubts.

V. Be Willing to Study

People often see and hear objections to the Christian faith. The evidences of Christianity, however, they do not know, and they may not have even heard the subject mentioned from the pulpit. Doubt is created in the back of their minds and they become somewhat uneasy. Someone may then introduce them to a treatise on Christian evidence, but it may seem too long and difficult to read. And, futhermore, they may even wonder whether or not there is something to the objections to Christianity since it takes much space to answer it. They thus remain in ignorance of the answer to the objections, but the objections keep preying on their minds. What shall we say to this?

Those who are willing to be honest will be willing to wait for the answer to the objection even if it takes some time to give a complete and satisfactory answer. To raise the question, or the doubt; and to demand an explanation; and then to run away, so to speak, because it takes a little time and effort to give and to get the answer is certainly unfair and indicates a certain carelessness to the claims of truth.

"But," a person may reply, "why should it take so long to give an answer?" There are many objections to the Christian faith which can be answered briefly; there are others, however, which involve either a long process of reasoning, or the massing of a great deal of evidence. It should be easy to understand that although a question may be asked in ten words it may take many more than that to answer it. For example, a person could ask: Please explain to me in a few simple words how the atomic bomb works? It would take a book, or thereabouts, and unless the individual was willing to study he still would not get it. We do not imply that most questions concerning the Christian faith would be that complicated, but we are illustrating the fact that a question may take only a few words, but that it cannot always be answered in as few words as it is asked. An objection to the Christan faith, or a misrepresentation of it, may be stated in a paragraph or a page but the answer to that objection may take a number of pages. He who takes the time to ask the question, or state the objection, should be fair and love the truth enough to examine closely the answer.

The fact that objections can be raised easier than they can be answered implies that it takes more time to answer objections than to state them. Thus, the believer should recognize that he ought not to be hasty and reject the whole or part of Christianity because he cannot find immediately an answer to some particular objection. Furthermore, when he does find the objection refuted he should not become impatient because it takes some time and thought in order to follow the argument, or arguments, which are set forth in answer to the objection. Here haste indeed makes waste as it may lead one to reject Christianity and waste his life and soul.

VI. THE FAILURE TO RECOGNIZE WHEN A THING IS PROVED

Unbelievers sometimes feel confident in their unbelief simply because they have failed to understand when a thing is proved. Laboring under a misconception on this score they continue to call for proof of Christianity long after the case for Christianity has been well established. When dealing with Christianity, but not as a general rule when they are dealing with other things, *they act as if Christianity cannot be established unless and until no possible additional objections can be brought against it.* So as long as they can raise objections they think that they have razed Christianity.

There is nothing which is objection-proof. Controversy has raged on every subject. There are some who will object to the simple fact that you are standing before them and addressing them. In a conversation with a Christian Scientist the author's remarks concerning Christian Science were met with the statement that: "You are not here." Dr. Johnson well said that "there are objections against a *plenum* ('a space that is filled, or conceived as being filled, with matter'), and objections against a *vacuum;* but one of them must be true." There are objections against any freedom of the will, and there are objections against determinism, and yet one of them must be true. A skilled lawyer can bring objections against testimony, truthful testimony, given by a witness in court. Dr. Richard Whately has brought a number of plausible objections against the existence of Napoleon, in his book on *Historic Doubts Relating to Napoleon,* and yet few if any doubt that Napoleon once existed.

"One does not reject the majority of principles and facts with which he is confronted, just because someone can raise objections, even plausible ones, to them. To do so would be to act as if there could not be truth, and truth supported by irrefragable arguments, and yet at the same time obnoxious to objections, numerous, plausible, and by no means easy of solution."[7]

Unbelievers often act on this recognition when dealing with things other than the claims of Christ, so why should they abandon such an obvious and well known principle when dealing with His credentials? Why do they allow their objections to hide from their view the mountain of truth which supports Christianity? If the reader is not a believer in Christ we kindly entreat him to weigh carefully the claims and credentials of Christianity and not cast it overboard because difficulties and objections can still be raised after the evidence of Christianity has been studied. Recognize and act on the fact that a principle or fact can be proved without dealing with all possible objections.

---

[7]Dr. Hawkins, *Essay on Tradition,* Quoted by Richard Whately, *Elements of Logic,* p. 428 (Boston: James Munroe and Co., 1854).

CHAPTER IV

CONDITIONS OF HEART WHICH FRUSTRATE FAITH

Jesus knew the pyschological make-up of man and thus He knew what would thwart and what would promote the growth of faith. In the parable of the sower He has shown us that not merely the nature of the seed sown, but also the condition of the soil into which the seed falls, will determine whether or not fruit will be brought forth. The parable is, among other things, an explanation of why all did not accept Jesus' message. And it placed the responsibility for the wrong condition of the heart on man himself.

The proof that this parable is an explanation of why all men do not believe is found not only in Jesus' reference, which we shall quote in a moment, concerning the condition of their hearts in general, but it is also shown by the explanation of the parable itself. Jesus said: "Therefore speak I to them in parables; because seeing they see not, and hearing they hear not, neither do they understand. And unto them is fulfilled the prophecy of Isaiah, which saith: By hearing we shall hear, and shall in no wise understand; and seeing ye shall see, and shall in no wise perceive; *for* (and this is the reason, J. D. B.) this people's heart is waxed gross, and their ears are dull of hearing, and their eyes they have closed: lest happily they should perceive with their eyes, and hear with their ears, and understand with their heart, and should turn again, and I should heal them. But blessed are your eyes, for they see: and your ears, for they hear . . . Hear then ye the parable of the sower. When any one heareth the word of the kingdom, and understandeth it not, then cometh the evil one, and snatcheth away that which has been sown in his heart. This is he that was sown by the way side. And he that was sown upon the rocky places, this is he that heareth the word, and straight-way with joy receiveth it; yet hath he not root in himself, but endureth for a while; and when tribulation or persecution ariseth because of the word, straightway he stumbleth. And he that was sown among the thorns, this is he that heareth the word: and the care of the world, and the deceitfulness of riches, choke the word, and he becometh unfruitful. And he that was sown upon the good ground, this is he that heareth the word, and understandeth it: who verily beareth fruit, and bringeth forth, some an hundredfold, some sixty, some thirty." (Matt, 13:13-23). Let us examine this parable and show how that the various con- ditions of heart may keep people from examining and under- standing the word. And these conditions will continue as long as they are willing for them to continue. If and when they become willing they, too, can understand and obey the word.

I. THE HEART WHICH HEARS NOT

It is possible for an individual to become so engrossed in some things that he fails to see other things. For example, one who is engrossed in a book, or a certain piece of research, may not hear the noise around him, and may have to be addressed several times before he becomes conscious that someone has spoken to him. This, of course, is very helpful provided that an individual does not fail to hear and to do those things which are most needful for life. It is possible to become so engrossed that one fails to see the good or to heed the danger which is before him. People have walked into telephone poles because they were engrossed in something and failed to notice where they were going. Pre-occupation, when overdone, can become an enemy to the development of character and spirituality.

There are people who become so engrossed in some small area of scientific investigation that everything else becomes un- important and somewhat unreal for them. Through years of con- centration on matter and its relationship they may be led to con- clude that matter is all that exists, and yet in this very instance it has been mind and not matter which has been intently study- ing matter. Other things may be neglected until he no longer responds to things which once fascinated him. Darwin wrote that "Up to the age of thirty or beyond it, poetry of many kinds gave me great pleasure; and even as a schoolboy I took intense delight in Shakespeare especially in the historical plays. I have also said that pictures formerly gave me considerable, and music very great delight. But now for many years I cannot endure to read a line of poetry. I have tried lately to read Shakespeare, and found it so intolerably dull that it nauseated me. I have also almost lost my taste for pictures or music. . . .my mind seems to have become a kind of machine for grinding general laws out of large collections of facts; but why this should have caused the atrophy of that part of the brain alone, on which the higher tastes depend, I cannot conceive. . . If I had to live my life again, I would have made a rule to read some poetry and listen to some music at least once every week; for perhaps the part of my brain now atrophied would thus have been kept alive through use. The loss of these tastes is a loss of happiness, and may possibly be injurious to the intellect, and more probably to the moral character, by enfeebling the emotional part of our nature."

John Locke, who recognized that "the works of nature are contrived by a wisdom" which surpasses our faculties to conceive completely, stated as follows that truth which we are considering. "Because matter being a thing that all our senses are constantly conversant with, it is so apt to possess the mind, and exclude all other things but matter, that prejudice, grounded on such principles, often leaves no room for the admittance of spirits, or the allowing any such things as immaterial beings. . . when yet it is evident, that by mere matter and motion, none of the great phenomena of nature can be resolved."[1]

Tyndall, by no means a believer in the Bible, recognized this truth when he pointed out that the devotion of a life to a different classes of ideas, and he had reference to a particular scientist, "tended rather him less instead of more competent to deal with theological and historic questions." [2]

This pre-occupation may be centered not only in science, but in social relationships; business; the pursuit of wealth; or anything else which so fills one's mind that nothing which is not in line

---

[1] J. W. Adamson, *The Educational Writings of John Locke*, p. 160.
[2] *Fragments of Science*, Vol. II, p. 150.

with it can enter. What the mind is filled with and set on determines what the mind will see. It will tend to pass over all that is
foreign to its desire and purpose. What it does take in it construes
in terms of its own interests and purpose. Because it has no desire
for the spiritual, because it considers the religious to be of no value,
it passes by without any adequate examination. It is unwilling
to bother with it for it is foreign to what the person has in mind
to accomplish in life.

Some live in such a hurry that they are robbing themselves of
an opportunity to study seriously the goal of life. When questions
concerning God; the origin and the destiny of life; of the meaning of life; arise in their consciousness they impatiently brush
them aside and busy themselves about other things. They are too
busy to try to meet the deeper needs of their own nature.

The effect, on one's attitude toward life and God, of so
much ceaseless hustle and bustle has been well stated by Alvin
Hobby. "Life in all its phases has been speeded up to such a
degree that it is hard for the average person even to keep up.
Like an incident in *Alice in Wonderland,* you have to run as
hard as you can and keep on running just to stay where you are!

"Consequently, we are in a hurry from the cradle to the
grave. We are always wishing for tomorrow or next week—just
any time but the present. This is a fast age, and we have to
keep up some way, somehow, and even push things a little sometimes. If we don't, we'll soon get hopelessly behind. The sign at
the railroad crossing reads, 'Stop! Look! Listen! Instead we skip,
hop, and hasten! And many of our proverbs have necessarily
been changed and given a modern version. 'We never do today
that which can be put off until tomorrow.'

"This hurry and uneasiness soon becomes a part of us. To
a certain extent, it carries over to our 'recreation,' and we are
not content unless we are on the run all the time. This soon leads
to intemperance in general. There are so many places to go and
so many things to do that we find it hard to get to bed before
eleven o'clock any night: and many times it is much later. Then,
after a few hours of sleep we arise with a bad case of 'the morn-

ing-after' feeling, a bad temper, and a bad taste for humanity in general.

"But, it's a great life—for awhile! Matters soon go from bad to worse because many seem to think that the best way to forget the effects of one drunk is to get on another. But the things we follow for pleasure, if carried to excess, may soon become actually boresome to us, so that we try to change from one thing to another, until we come to the realization of the fact that we have set a pace that we cannot maintain without disastrous results both physically and mentally: and then we are downright miserable. We are disgusted with life: everything goes wrong: and nothing really matters any longer.

"It is said that misery likes company, and this is likely true. So, in a feeble attempt to justify our wretched condition and give our dying consciences a little ease, we try to place the whole world on a level with us. Nobody is honest. Everybody is a cheat and a pickpocket—if given a chance, and has a selfish motive for everything he does. And then, as a final step, we kill our dying consciences (if not already dead) and dispense with all moral and spiritual obligations and responsibilities simply by saying that all religion is so much bunk and that 'Our Father who is in heaven is dead'."[3]

This is the type of heart that Jesus referred to in the parable of the sower as the wayside hearer. "*The wayside hearer* hears the word, but does not understand it,—or, to use a phrase which expresses at once the literal and the figurative truth, does not take it in. Thoughtlessness, spiritual stupidity, arising not so much from want of intellectual capacity as from preoccupation of mind, is the characteristic. . .Their mind is like a footpath beaten hard by the constant passage through it of 'the wishes of the flesh and the current thoughts' concerning common earthly things. For a type of the class we may take the man who interrupted Christ while preaching on one occasion, and said: 'Master, speak to my brother, that he divide the inheritance with me.' (Lk. 12:13). He had just heard Christ utter the words, 'And when they bring

---

[3]*The Plan of Salvation for a Modern Generation.* Quoted from the manuscript.

you unto the synagogues, and unto magistrates and powers,'
(Lk. 12:11), and these suggested to him the topic on which his
thoughts were habitually fixed—his dispute with his brother
about their patrimony. And so it happened to him according to
the parable. The truth he had heard did not get into his mind,
hardened as it was like a beaten path by the constant passage
through it of current thoughts about money: it was very soon
forgotten altogether, caught away by the god of this world, who
ruled over him through his covetous disposition. It may be regarded as certain that there were many such hearers in the crowd
by the lake,—men in whose minds the doctrine of the kingdom
merely awakened hopes of worldly prosperity,—who, as Jesus
afterwards told them, laboured for the meat that perisheth, not
for the meat that endureth unto everlasting life. (John 2:27).
Such were they who 'received seed by the wayside'."[4] As Arnot said: "The place is a thoroughfare; a mixed multitude
of this worlds affairs tread over it from day to day, and from year
to year. It is not fenced like a garden, but exposed like an un-
cultivated common. That secret of the Lord, 'Enter into thy closet,'
and 'shut the door', is unknown: or if known, neglected. The soil,
trodden by all comers, is never broken up and softened by a
thorough self-searching. A human heart may thus become marvel-
lously callous both to good and evil. The terrors of the Lord and
the tender invitations of the Gospel are alike ineffectual. Falling
only upon the external senses, they are swept off by the next
current; as the solid grain thrown from the sower's hand rattles
on the smooth hard road side, and lies on the surface till the fowls
carry it away."[5]

And thus the heart is so preoccupied that it does not try
to understand the message. "He does not recognize himself as
standing in any relation to the word which he hears, or to the
kingdom of grace which that word proclaims. All that speaks of
man's connection with a higher invisible world, all that speaks of

    [4]Alexander Balmain Bruce, *The Parabolic Teaching of Christ*, New
York: A. C. Armstrong and Son, 1886, pp. 25-26.

    [5]William Arnot, *The Parables of Our Lord*, London: T. Nelson and
Sons, 1867, p. 52.

sin, of redemption, of holiness, is unintelligible to him, and without, significance."[6]

This danger is not only one to which non-christians are exposed, but also Christians if they are not careful. One may listen to the word that is preached, or read the Bible, simply as a mere form and never apply or meditate on what he has read. "The soul may be sermon-hardened, as well as sin-hardened. One may get into the habit of having the verities of the gospel presented to him, and resisted by him, that by and by he takes no note whatever of what is said by the preacher, and it falls on the outside of him, like rain upon a rock, or snow upon a roof. There is little danger of this, perhaps, in an age or in a place in which gospel privileges are rare, but it becomes very real and insidious in days like our own, when these blessings are so commonly and so regularly enjoyed; and there are too many in all our congregations like Tennysons 'Northern Farmer' of the old school, who said about the parson,—

'And I always came to his church, before my Sally were dead,
And heard him a-bumming away like a buzzard-clock over my head;
And I never knew what he meant, but I thought he had something to say,
And I thought he said what he ought to have said, and I came away.'

"This is a very serious peril, and has to be strenuously looked after, especially by those who have from their early years been constant attendants on the sanctuary. The preacher may do much to counteract it, indeed, by cultivating fresh methods of presenting and enforcing the truth, and by adjuring all stereotyped phraseology in his discourses: but the hearer, also must use means to neutralize it, and should seek to stir up his attention when he enters the place of worship, by pausing a little to ask himself why he is there, and to lift up his heart in prayer to God, for the open ear to hear, and the open heart to receive, the message which his Lord has, in his providence, prepared for him."[7]

---

[6] R. C. Trench, *Notes on the Parables of Our Lord*, London: George Routledge and Sons, Limited, p. 57.

[7] William M. Taylor, *The Parables of Our Saviour*, New York: George H. Doran Company, 1886, pp. 25-26.

To fail to recognize and avoid this danger may lead one to become involved in such a sense of the unreality of Christianity, a feeling that it is composed of mere words, that he may finally drift away from it and repudiate it.

The person who allows his thinking to be so dominated by things of this world that he refuses to think on the purpose of life: the longing of his own spiritual nature which may manifest itself from time to time only to be ignored or thwarted; and to weigh the claims of religion; has placed himself under the influence of the evil one to the extent that for the time being he has access to the person's heart and through evil thoughts, passions, lusts, and various forms of preoccupations, snatcheth away the seed. For this the individual is responsible since the weapons which Satan is using against him are weapons which he himself has placed in the devils hands. Only because he is willing to have it that way does the devil have such easy access to his heart. When he is willing to have it otherwise, he can hear and heed the word of the kingdom.

II. The Shallow, Unthinking Individual

"Moving with the tide", fitly characterizes the lives of some individuals. When the tide flows in favor of religion, when their crowd is going that way, they go that way. When the crowd turns, they turn with it. They are the ones who receive the word but who have no root in themselves and when difficulties arise because of the word they reject the word. "The characteristic of this class is emotional, excitability, inconsiderate, impulsiveness. They receive the word readily with joy; but without thought. The latter trait is not indeed specified, but it is clearly implied in the remark concerning the effect of tribulation, persecution, or temptation on this class of hearers. They had not anticipated such experiences, they did not count the cost, there was a want of deliberation at the commencement of their religious life, and by implication a want of that mental constitution which ensures that there shall be deliberation, that is the fault of the class now under consideration, not the mere fact of their receiving the word with joy. . .the joy of the good and honest heart is a thoughtful joy, associated with and springing out of the exercise of the in-tellectual and moral powers upon the truth believed. The joy of the stony ground hearer, on the contrary, is a thoughtless joy coming to him through the effects of what he hears upon the imagination and the feelings. Joy without thought is his definition.

"Of course a religious experience of this character cannot last; it is doomed to prove abortive. For tribulation, persecution, temptation in some form, will come, not to be withstood except by those whose whole spiritual being—mind, heart, conscience—is influenced by the truth: and even by them only by the most strenuous exertion of their moral energies. A man who has been touched only on the surface of his soul by a religious movement, who has been impressed on the sympathetic side of his nature by a prevalent enthusiasm, and has yielded to the current without understanding what it means, whither it tends, and what it in-volves,—such a man has no chance of persevering under the conditions of trial amidst which the divine life has to be lived in this world. He is doomed to be scandalised by tribulation, to apostatise in the season of temptation. For he hath not root in *himself,* in his moral personality, in the faculties constituting personality—the reason, conscience, and will—which remain hard, untouched, unpenetrated by the fibres of his faith: his root is in others, in a prevalent popular enthusiasm: his religion is a thing of sympathetic imitation. He is not only— temporary, but likewise in the sense of being a creation of the time, a child of the *zeitgeist.* He comes forth as a professor of religion 'at the call of a shallow enthusiasm, and through the epidemic influence of a popular cause.' And this fact largely explains his temporariness. When the tide of enthuasiasm subsides, and he is left to himself to carry on single-handed the struggle with temptation, he has no heart for the work, and his religion withers away, like the corn growing on rocky places under the scorching heat of the summer sun."[8]

As Welsh pointed out, unbelief sometimes becomes the fash-ion; just as it is sometimes fashionable to believe. "One observes how commonly professed belief in Christianity is a matter of

[8]A. B. Bruce, *op. cit.,* pp. 26-27.

mere social fashion and traditional convention, not hypocritical, but imitative and superficial. Equally may men's minds be caught by an epidemic of doubt, falling victim to a social vogue or disbelief. Is there not a social infection of scepticism, a craze for questioning, abroad today?

> 'Had I been born three hundred years ago,
> They'd say, "What's strange? Blougram of course believes."
> And, seventy years since, "disbelieves *of course.*"
> But now, "He may believe: and yet—and yet—
> How can he?" '

"In estimating the significance of present-day unbelief, we have to recall the fact that the same infection visited Britain during the latter part of the seventeenth, and again of the eighteenth century. May it not be a recurrent epidemic? A century ago Voltaire, Rousseau, and the French Encyclopaedists killed the Christain religion. Voltaire pronounced it dead. But the room where he penned its obituary afterwards became a Bible Depot. How many lives this faith of Jesus has shown that it possesses! Its power of Resurrection, its power to outlive perversions and criticism, is surely a sign that in it lies the Truth eternal. Just when our modern prophets are declaring that the old faith is losing its hold, it is commanding more of the general intelligence of the world, and displaying more activity all around our globe, than it has done in any century of the past. 'The lesson of life,' says Emerson, 'is to believe what the years and the centuries say against the hours'."[9]

III. CHRISTIANITY CROWDED OUT

The wayside heart never gave the word an opportunity because its attention was centered on other things. The thorny heart is somewhat like it, not that it did not receive the word, but that it later permitted the word to become crowded out. It may be crowded out because of the wrong attitude toward life's riches or life's cares: or (as recorded in Luke 8:14) by the cares, riches, and pleasures of this life. It may seem strange that such different things can result in the same consequences. "But the

---

[9] *In Relief of Doubt,* pp. 35-37.

Lord, in fact, here presents to us this earthly life on its two sides, under its two aspects. There is, first, its crushing oppressive side, the poor man's toil how to live at all, to keep hunger and naked-ness from the door, and struggle for a daily subsistence, 'the cares of this life,' which, if not met in faith, hinder the thriving of the spiritual word in the heart. But life has its flattering as well as its threatening side, its pleasures not less than its cares; and as those who have heard and received the word of the kingdom with gladness are still in danger of being crushed by the cares of life, so, no less, of being deceived by its flatteries and its allure-ments."[10] "Both from our own experience in the world and the specific terms employed by the Lord in the interpretation of the parable, we learn that all classes and all ranks are on this side exposed to danger. This is not a rich man's business, or a poor man's; it is every man's business. The words point to the two extremes of worldly condition, and include all that lies between them. 'The care of the world' becomes the snare of those who have little, and 'the deceitfulness of riches,' the snare of those who have much. Thus the world wars against the soul, alike when it smiles and when it frowns. Rich and poor have in this matter no room and no right to cast stones at each other. Pinching want and luxurious profusion are, indeed, two widely diverse species of thorns; but when favoured by circumstances they are equally rank in their growth and equally effective in destroying the precious seed."[11]

Our time and attention are limited. When we allow corrod-ing cares to paralyze the mind and to hide from us the spiritual; or the deceitfulness of riches to render the spiritual tasteless and undesirable; we are of the thorny ground which chokes to death the word of God so that it does not bring forth fruit in our life.

This does not mean that an individual deliberately decides to repudiate Christianity; no, far from it. He does not carefully examine the evidences of Christianity; consider clearly the con-sequences of such a rejection; and then renounce the faith. He

---

[10]R. C. Trench, op. cit., pp. 62-63.
[11]William Arnot, op. cit., p. 63.

simply lets other things crowd and choke it. An analogy drawn from physical life may enable this to be seen more clearly. There are many physical wrecks in this world who never set out to be physical wrecks. No one convinced them, by a series of arguments, that health is highly undesirable and that sickness is the state of life which is highly to be desired. All that they had to do, to become physical wrecks, was to neglect those things which are necessary to health and to drift into those habits which undermine health. Just so, those represented as the thorny ground do not necessarily listen to, or become convinced by, arguments against the Christian faith. They simply neglect the cultivation of the spiritual life; they permit the word—and meditation on it and practice of it—to be crowded out of their lives; and they end up spiritual wrecks. This, we are persuaded, is the case with a large percentage of the individuals who lose faith. In fact, they and those represented by the stony ground constitute the overwhelming majority of those who have lost faith.

IV. THE GOOD AND HONEST HEART

The person with the good and honest heart is not already a Christian. He is the person, however, who wants to do good and is honest and thus willing to admit; to accept; and act on the truth when he sees it. His "aim is noble" and he "is generously devoted to his aim." His mind is "raised above moral vulgarity, and is bent, not on money-making and such low pursuits, but on the attainment of wisdom, holiness, righteousness." He wants to do the good and is willing to listen to the truth although it may try his soul and call on him for effort and sacrifice. Taylor well characterized this type of heart as possessing the following qualities which enable it to profit by the word. "The qualities which such hearts bring to the hearing of the gospel are these: Attention: they hear. Meditation: they keep. Obedience: they bring forth fruit with patience."[12]

In addition to the things which we have already mentioned, there are certain other psychological factors which are favor-

---

[12]*Op. cit.,* p. 34.

able to the growth of unbelief. The first one of these which we shall mention deals with the way in which vague rumors can contribute to unbelief.

V. Rumors Ruin When Bias Is Built Up

Vague rumors may instill doubts into some minds and upset them because of their threatening nature. "Vague hints that learned men have objected to such and such things, and have questioned this or that, often act like an inward slow-corroding canker in the minds of some who have never read or heard anything distinct on the subject; and who, for that very reason, are apt to imagine these objections, etc., to be much more formidable than they really are. For there are people of perverse mind, who, really possessing both learning and ingenuity, will employ these to dress up in a plausible form something which is, in truth, perfectly silly: and the degree to which this is sometimes done, is what no one can easily conceive without actual experience and examination. . . . .I know that many persons are a good deal influenced by reports and obscure rumors of the opinions of some supposed learned and able men, without knowing distinctly what they are; and are likely to be made uneasy and distrustful by being assured that this or that has been disputed, and so and so maintained by some person of superior knowledge and talents, who has proceeded on 'rational' grounds; when perhaps they themselves are qualified, by their own plain sense, to perceive how irrational these fanciful notions are, and to form a right judgement on the matter in question.[18]

These vague suspicions may gradually build up a bias against the Bible and so weaken faith that it may easily be upset by some great sorrow, or fall victim to the desires and inclinations of the individual to sin. It is necessary therefore for an individual, who has been disturbed by these things, to settle the doubts which have been raised by examining the rumors and the foundation on which they are based. He will find, as has been the

---

[18]Richard Whately, *A View of the Scripture Revelations Respecting Good and Evil Angels* (Philadelphia: Lindsay and Blakiston, 1856), pp. 74-75.

experience of the writer, that the "reasons" on which the
"learned" men have based their objections to the Bible are not
nearly so reasonable or convincing as they try to make them
appear. Often no more is necessary to dispel the doubt than a
clear statement of the reasons on which the person based his
objections. The author well remembers reading a book by a
famous scholar, Dr. Goodspeed, in which objections were offered to Paul's authorship of a certain epistle. A mere reading
of his arguments was enough to see their absurdity if a person
read without his eyes being blinded by certain irrational assumptions. The only word the writer could find to express his verdict
was: "Bosh."

One should not, however, meet the doubts which are in
the minds of others with such an expression. He must show,
not merely say, that it is bosh. Or he must show, in some cases, that
the difficulties which are involved are not such as to undermine
faith. To fail to do so is to add another burden to a faith which
is already weak. This is sometimes done when one answers the
question of a believer, who is having difficulty with some things
in the Bible, by saying that he must believe it because the Bible
says it. This answer is sufficient *when the individual has been
fully assured on other grounds that the Bible is the word of God.*
When he has a number of reasons for the hope which is within
him, when he has strong faith in the Bible, it will not harm his
faith to give such an answer. If, on the other hand, the person
is weak in the faith and has never examined carefully the field
of Christian evidence, the difficulty in the Bible is a strain on his
weak faith. And to say that he must believe it just because the
Bible says so is not enough since the thing itself is weakening
his faith in the Bible. Do not overload a weak faith. One should
deal with the difficulty and show that it is not an obstacle to
faith in the Bible. In many cases it will be possible to show the
objection is based on a misunderstanding or a misrepresentation
of the Bible. When the explanation is given that particular difficulty to the person's faith is removed and his faith becomes
stronger.[14]

---

[14]R. E. D. Clark, *Conscious and Unconscious Sin*, pp. 157-159.

The following quotation from Dr. Green, concerning Bishop Colenso, seems to indicate that a failure to deal with doubts as they arose; the crowding of them into the back of the mind; and then trying to face them without being aware of the bias that this process had built up against the faith; was one of the reasons that he lost faith. "Now, we have no idea that anything which we, or anyone else, can say in reply to the like objections which Bishop Colenso has brought against the Pentateuch will alter the state of his mind, or that of others like-minded with him. The difficulty is in the whole attitude which he occupies. He has picked out a few superficial difficulties in the sacred record, not now adduced for the first time, not first discovered by himself. They seem, however, to have recently dawned upon his view. He was aware, long before, of certain difficulties in the scriptural account of the creation and deluge; and instead of satisfactorily and thoroughly investigating these, he was content, he tells us, to push them off, or thrust them aside, satisfying himself with the moral lessons, and trusting vaguely, and, as he owns, not very honestly (p. 47), that there was some way of explaining them (pp. 4-5). The other difficulties, which have since oppressed him, he then had no notion of; in fact, so late as the time when he published or prepared his Commentary on the Romans (p. 215) he had no idea of ever holding his present view. As there is nothing brought out in his book which un-believers have not flaunted and believing expositors set them-selves to explain long since, we are left to suppose that his theological training as a minister and a bishop, and his preparation as a commentator, could not have been very exact or thorough. If the Pentateuch is the book of absurdities he asserts, and these are so palpable as he asserts, and yet he never saw it or imagined it until now, his wits must have been recently sharpened, or his acquaintance with the book of which he was a professed teacher and expounder must have been limited indeed."[15] The bias built by a failure to deal honestly with his first difficulties left him in no frame of mind which would enable him to be victorious over

---

[15]W. H. Green, *The Pentateuch Vindicated From the Aspersions of Bishop Colenso*, New York: John Wiley, 1863, pp. 11-12.

additional difficulties; especially if he began to look for them
and gathered a whole lot of them at once. A faith already
weakened by difficulties which he had concluded could not be
solved, was certainly in no position to bear a large number of
other difficulties.

VI. A Bias Created by Faulty Reading in Christian Evidence

The first glance that the unbeliever takes at a work on
Christian evidence will not dissolve his doubt. In fact, a hasty
scanning of a book on the subject may tend to increase his infidelity since it in the author will state, and answer, a good
many objections which have never occurred to the unbelieving
scanner. These may strike him by their novelty; because they are
right in line with his present state of mind; and because it is
easier to see the objection, when briefly stated, than the answer
which may take some time. It may take, in fact it generally will,
some time and effort to attend closely to the answers and to
weigh them fairly.

Dr. Nelson, who was once an infidel, made a similar observation and then pointed out the cure. "An infidel, when
he begins to read on the evidences of Christianity, becomes more
doubting and sceptical than ever, or more confirmed in his unbelief. This continues to increase during the former part of the
research; but let him persevere in a thorough investigation, and
he begins to have a view of the truth, and is at last delivered
altogether from the thraldom of the delusion. The facts are ac-
curately pictured by the words of the much worn expression
concerning the Pierian spring: the same waters that at first
intoxicate, will sober again if drank plentifully. Many who begin
to read, after glancing through one or two volumes hastily, lay
them aside more entangled in error than they were and thinking
within themselves that they have read the strongest arguments
that can be brought forward in favor of divine inspiration. Their
condition is of course more deplorable than it was. Others do
hastily examine a few volumes and are not well enough informed

to be able to understand clearly, and fairly weigh the arguments of the author; these may desist before they have mastered the subject. Others may need a second or third perusal of the same pages before they can clearly view and appropriate the contents. Such may fancy that they have examined the subject, when they really have not. But of those who have read six or eight authors on that subject, clearly, attentively, impartially, industriously, and renewedly if necessary, I have never known one who did not cast away his infidelity. If anyone should ask why we request the unbeliever to read many authors on the same subject, the *evidences of Christianity,* we answer, that no two minds take the same course in writing on this subject. The arguments and evidences could not be condensed or abridged into a score of large volumes. Of course each writer is expected merely to select such ideas as strike him most forcible (or which are in line with the particular phase of the subject on which he is writing and the specific objection which he is answering, J. D. B.). True, I have never read the author on the evidences of Christianity who did not seem to me in some one way or another to establish the position, *This is God's book*: but the further we push our re-searches, meditations, and inquiries, the more readily can we proceed, and the more capable are we of comprehending additional research. The case is by no means an uncommon one, where a reader lays down an author on this subject with disappoint-ment and dissatisfaction, finding it, as seems to him, very little excellence of any kind. Twelve months after, upon taking up casually the same volume, he is astonished at a thought there which he had not noticed before. He proceeds, and many of the arguments there appear as clear and distinct as a stream of electricity over a dark cloud. The reason of this is, that his mind is in a condition better to perceive, weight and prize the argu-ment. His mind becomes thus better capable while reading other things on the same subject in other writers."[16]

---

[16]Dr. David Nelson, *The Cause and Cure of Infidelity,* New York: George H. Doran Company, pp. 130-132.

VII. The Psychological Reaction of a Faulty Expectation

There are individuals who made a profession of faith, but who have given it up after maintaining that it did not work for them. This is due to a misunderstanding of the nature of the faith. Through false teaching, teaching which is not sustained by the Bible but which some have taught because they were ig-norant of the Bible, some individuals have been led to expect that when they believe and are saved that God will send them some sort of feeling. When they do everything that they are told to do, by those who are teaching them this type of error, and they do not feel any different they give up and maintain that Chris-tianity does not work for them.

The Bible does not teach that a person gets a certain feeling as the evidence that he has been accepted by God. It is true that a Christian ought to have a peace of heart and mind but this is produced by his confidence in the word of God. Feelings flow from the faith; feeling does not produce the faith. The apostles of Christ presented the credentials of Christ and on the basis of these credentials told the people that they could know assuredly that God had made Jesus both Lord and Christ and that by Him the world was to be judged (Acts 2:38; 17:31). The faith which is based on these credentials is a full assurance that what God has promised He is able to perform, and thus the Christian feels good because of his confidence in God's word. But he does not regard the feeling as a sign that Chris-tianity is really working for him.

When one has obeyed the gospel, and has the full assur-ance of faith (based on God's word) that God has pardoned him, Christianity also works for him in the sense that he continues his obedience and instills its principles into life. He does not lie down and expect the principles of the Christian life to work for him without any effort of his own, but he finds that its principles work when put to work in one's life. The proof of the pudding is in the eating thereof, and through walking by Christian principles the individual increasingly realizes that they go in the right direction; that they meet the deep spiritual needs of man; and that they develop men as does nothing else. In this way he finds that Christianity works.

VIII. A Psychological Reaction to a Feeling of Unreality

In speaking of Jesus as the Word, John said that the Word was made flesh and dwelt among us (John 1:14). In a different sense this must become true of each believer if he is to remain a believer. The words of Jesus Christ must become the guide of our life. Unless we let the word become flesh in us, that is, make it the way of life, we are apt to lose faith in it because it becomes unreal to us. The man who recites one thing with his lips on the Lord's day in the church service; but whose life speaks not only a foreign language but one which is also antagonistic to the Christian life, cannot long cling, with any measure of feeling of reality, to the shell of his faith. The person who does not speak some word for Christ both in defense and propagation of his faith, at some time or other; the person who does not test the principles of holiness by walking in them; the person who does not visit the sick and otherwise exercise Christian compassion; the person who does not study his Bible; pray to God; and thus do those things which are part and parcel of the Christian life; will finally give up in despair because Christianity does not have the ring of reality to him. It becomes vague to him, unreal, intangible, and thus more and more difficult to profess even lip-service to it. That which is denied by our everyday life cannot always remain the object of real faith. Thus one must remember in thought and deed that " 'nothing is so inimical to Christian belief, as unchristian conduct.' (G. J. Romanes). If faith is to be retained, it must bring life into harmony with itself."[17]

IX. The Result of Continuous Verbalization

Those, however, who do not renounce religion may continue verbalizing—saying the words of religion without giving their hearts to God. Their inward failure to submit to God is never-

---

[17]John Reid, *op. cit.*, p. 41.

theless revealed sooner or later. When an obligation from God is placed on them, which is contrary to their desires and ambitions their accompanying rebellion brings to the surface the fact that they have been rendering a lip-service instead of a life-service. Of this type of individual, with whom He was confronted in His ministry, Jesus said: "But I know you, that ye have not the love of God in you. I am come in my Father's name, and ye receive me not: if another shall come in his own name, him ye will receive. How can ye believe, which receive honor one of another, and seek not the honor that cometh from God only?" (John 5:42-44)

On these verses Meyer paraphrased and commented as follows: "I do not utter these reproaches against you from (disappointed) ambition, but because I have perceived what a want of all right feeling towards God lies at the root of your unbelief." "If they *had love to God* in their hearts (this being the summary of their law), they would have felt sympathy towards the Son, whom the Father (Ver. 43) sent, and would and received and recognized Him . . . love to God . . . was an excellence *foreign* to them, of which *they themselves* were destitute—a mere theory, *existing outside the range of their inner* life (Ver. 43)." A false prophet, Jesus said, you will receive. "*He* will be received, because he satisfies the opposite of the love of God, viz. *self-love* (by promising earthly glory, indulgence towards sin, etc.)."

In verse 44 "the reproach of unbelief now rises to its highest point, for Jesus in a wrathful question denies to the Jews even the *ability* to believe . . . the ground of this impossibility is: because ye *receive honour one of another* . . . because ye reciprocally give and take honour of yourselves. This ungodly desire of honour (comp. 12:43; Matt, 23:5 sqq.), and its necessarily accompanying indifference towards the true honour, which comes from God, must so utterly blight and estrange the heart from the divine element of life, that it is not even *capable* of faith."[18] For this incapacity they were responsible, and for its continuation they were responsible for had they been willing to humble themselves, and to seek God's will above all, rather than their

---

[18]*Commentary on John*, pp. 192-193.

own way, they would have prepared their hearts for the reception of the seed of the kingdom which Jesus was proclaiming.

X. Examples of the Bias of Some Unbelievers

Lest the reader conclude many unbelievers are thoughtful men who would not allow pre-conceptions to blind them to the weight of the evidences for Christianity it is well to show that such bias does operate. Three considerations show this. *First,* the discussions of various causes of unbelief, in this book, show that such pre-conceptions do operate. *Second,* even very intelligent men, who are able to think straight on many subjects, have blind spots, rationalized patches so to speak, in their minds which as long as they tolerate them will prevent them from clear thinking on certain subects. One does not have to associate very long with scientists or read very far in what some scientists write on subjects outside, and often inside, their fields to see that they, too, have some of the common failings of humanity, such as prejudice. *Third,* we shall present two examples of well known figures of the past who admitted certain violent, blind prejudices, *T. H. Huxley* wrote as follows of the writings of a fellow agnostic, Mr. Laing: " 'Polarity', in Article VIII, for example, is a word about which I heard a good deal in my youth, when 'Natur-philesphie' was in fashion, and greatly did I suffer from it. For many years past, whenever I have met with 'polarity' anywhere but in a discussion of some purely physical topic, such as magnetism, I have shut the book. Mr. Laing must excuse me if the force of habit was too much for me when I read his eighth article."[19] In other words, no argument which was advanced after such a word was used would have any affect on Huxley, *because he would not read far enough to get it.*

Herbert Spencer, one of the popularizers of evolution, spoke of one of his prejudices when he said: "My knowledge of Kant's writing is extremely limited. In 1844 a translation of his 'Critique of Pure Reason' (then I think lately published) fell into my hands, and I read the first few pages enunciating

---

[19]*Agnosticism and Christainity,* p. 44.

his doctrine of Time and Space: my peremptory rejection of which caused me to lay the book down. Twice since then the same thing has happened: *for, being an impatient reader, when I disagree with the cardinal propositions of a work I can go no further.*[20] Instead of so hastily rejecting a work, he should have examined more closely the cardinal propositions to see whether or not they were sustained in the main body of the work. And yet, a man who regarded himself as a scientist admitted that he was such an impatient reader that, in effect, he would not follow an argument through in a book if the cardinal propositions were not at once acceptable to him. And yet some people are so prejudiced that they assume that Christians are the people who are unwilling to think and to read material which is opposed to their principles.

Although the author is far from endorsing everything done or taught by many preachers, yet bias against any of them, because of evil which some of them have done, or the evil which some of them have condemned, should not lead one to ignore the truth. *Strauss* clearly stated the relationship of his bias against preachers and his antagonism toward miracles. "If we wish," he wrote, "to make progress in religious matters, then these theologians who stand above the prejudices and interests of the profession must go hand in hand with the thinking laymen in the Church. As soon as even the best among the people have made progress enough to refuse what the clergy still for the most part offer them, these latter will think better of it. When Christianity has ceased to be miraculous, they will no longer be able to pronounce blessings, but only to impart instruction (if Strauss or these preachers had known the New Testament they would have recognized that imparting instruction is the function of the teacher of the gospel; and that they are today in no way miracle-men able to give or withhold the blessings of God, J. D. B.); but it is well known that the latter of these occupations is as difficult and thankless as the former is easy and profitable.' (p.XII). Therefore, 'a pressure must be brought to bear on them by public opinion. But (and this is the only

---

[20]Quoted by Paul Carus, *Kant and Spencer*, pp. 71-72.

italicised sentence in the whole book) *whoever wishes to do away with the parsons in the Church, must first do away with the miracles in religion* (p. XIX)."[21] Christlieb comments as follows: "So this work, also, is but the means to a demagogue's ends, though not quite in the same manner as that of Schenkel. 'Our ultimate aim is not to ascertain the history of the past, but rather to help the human spirit in future to liberate itself from an oppressive yoke of belief' (p.XIV). Strauss' aim is 'not in the past, but in the future' (p.XV). He lays the axe at the root of the miraculous New Testament history, in order that, when this is done away with, the parsons may be abolished too. It is his wish to establish a free Church commonwealth, and to dissolve the different confessions into one great religion of humanity. We scarcely need to point out that this is only the effect of his old grudge against the theologians, who formerly, by their unanimous verdict against him, spoilt his career, and reduced him to the occupation of a literary man (cf. p.XIII). We see that this grudge has rather increased than decreased from the select names, such as 'field-mice,' 'rabble,' 'vermin,' which he bestows upon us biblical theologians (p. 6). Moreover, he declares that it is not worth his while 'to fight against such a rabble' as the recent apologists, because 'the conservation theology of the present day is wearying itself with the strangest contortions and the most venturesome caprioles,' and 'its paper battlements do not deserves a real siege' but yet he promises, 'for the sake of the joke, not entirely to give up doing so.' In all this, however, he forgets that *haughty contempt for the opponents* is everywhere the worst way to victory."[22]

From time to time one contacts unbelievers who are so biased that they assume that they are the only ones who can give the question of faith in God an unbiased study. But Wyckoff shows that such a one as Professor Leuba was not only biased but that this bias influenced his selection and treatment of data.

---

[21] Theodore Christlieb, *Modern Doubt and Christian Relief*, p. 385. Christlieb quoted from Strauss' *Life of Christ*, the first edition of 1864.

[22] *Ibid.*, p. 386.

Of course, if it be true that one cannot examine with any degree of fairness his own position, the position in which he believes, then the unbeliever is automatically disqualified from pronouncing a fair judgement on the grounds of his own belief. If he denies the ability of the believer to evaluate his own position he has accepted a principle which denies to the unbeliever himself the ability to evaluate *his* own position. But let us turn to the illustration presented by Wyckoff.

"In 1912, Professor Leuba published his book, entitled *A Psychological Study of Religion*. In this he frankly states that he does not believe in the existence of an objective God, and argues that this fact places him in a better position to study the whole subject, because, not being a believer, he is able to approach the subject from an entirely unprejudiced point of view." After the appearance of this book, Wyckoff was "so amazed at the arbitrary manner in which Professor Leuba rejected psychological data of great importance, that we wrote a series of articles entitled, *The Psychologist Among The Theologians,* and *The Theologians Among The Psychologists*. In these, we called attention to this unwarranted rejection of so much important data upon the subject of religion. Soon after the appearance of these articles, a letter was received from the previously mentioned friend of Mr. Cutter, telling the story of the questionnaire and asking if we would consent to understand the long delayed task of re-examining this material." The material here referred to was the material on which Leuba's doctor's dissertation had been based; the dissertation, however did not deal with the data in a manner which was satisfactory to the person who had helped gather the material. "The upshot of the whole matter is that we now have in our possession the original letters upon which Mr. Leuba based the conclusions found in his thesis on Religious Conversion. At some other time we hope to make a study of them. But our examination of this data reveals the fact that Professor Leuba adopted in this instance the same method which characterized his book. All of the data used are well analyzed, but the facts left out of his calculation are most significant. Some inhibitions clearly biased his selection of material. And these inhibitions were operating in the early years while he was still a student at Clarke University. No doubt Professor Leuba honestly believes that the conclusions which he states in his two recent books *A Psychological Study of Religion* and *The Belief in God and Immortality* are the inevitable resultants from the knowledge of psychology which he has gained during twenty-five years of thorough research. But as we shall see in a later chapter, every item of his anti-theistic and anti-Christian positions is contained in his maiden thesis writted at Clarke University in 1895. In other words, he was already an unbeliever before he began to investigate the psychological data of religious experience. And this attitude of unbelief was the dominant factor which controlled his selection and rejection of data."[23] And Leuba thought that being an unbeliever he was in a better position to deal with these matters!

XI. Overloading a Weak Faith

Unbelief is sometimes the result of the overloading of a weak faith. A person may be perplexed by something in the Bible, and instead of making an effort to get him to see the difficulty does not undermine faith in the Bible a teacher or friend may tell the individual that he must believe it because it is in the Bible. That is all right if the individual has studied enough to have a goodly number of reasons for his faith. If, however, he has never studied Christian Evidence very much, this difficulty may be shaking his faith in the Bible and thus it is not enough to tell him to believe it because it is in the Bible. The Bible itself is being called in question. And because he does not receive any reasonable help with his difficulty it may become one more stumbling block to a faith which is already weak. To be really helpful to someone with such a weak faith one must help him to see why he should believe the Bible and why the difficulty does not destroy the Bible.

Weak faith is also overloaded when doubt is met with the dogmatic assertion that one must believe all or nothing. This

[23]*Acute and Chronic Unbelief,* New York: Fleming H. Revell, 1924, pp. 32, 58-59.

does not give the individual any reason for believing the thing which is causing him difficulty and it tends to cast doubt on what he has aready accepted. "Mr. Froude once assured his readers in 'Good Words' (the articles are included in his Short Studies on Great Subjects, vol. iv.) that the Tractarian Move-ment, whilst headed by leaders of most devout spirit, made many sceptics among Oxford men, himself amongst the number. Mr. Lecky has been confirming this statement (Forum, June 1890). Newman and others virtually demanded 'Believe this or—nothing! In 'this' they included such points as seemed to baffle their com-prehension. Many courageous minds took them at their word. They strove to believe this, but having failed, 'Nothing be it then,' they exclaimed—and went away sorrowful."[24]

A weak faith is overloaded when all doubt is treated as if it is wicked. "Lord Chief Justice Coleridge, 'silver-tongue Cole-ridge,' once confessed to Keble that his mind was sorely perplexed on the question of Inspiration. Imagine the shock when he was told that 'most of the men who had difficulties on that subject were too wicked to be reasoned with.'

"Such a *wicked* retort may be taken as a short and easy way of making sceptics. To brand men's intelligent doubts as sins that incur perdition, must, if it do not frighten them out of all thinking, go far to force them into an attitude of definance and provide them with new reasons for doubt. Bradlaugh was driven from mere mental perplexity far towards stern disbelief by the snubbing meted out to him when he carried his questions to his clergyman. Men of conscious rectitude are embittered and aliena-ted by the insinuation that they are doubters because they are not good men, as surely as high-spirited horses are made frantic by the harsh use of bit and whip."[25] There are, as has been pointed out, those who are doubters because of their condition of heart; but there are also those whose doubt does not have that as its primary source. Jesus, as we shall show, did not condemn all doubt as sinful.

---

[24]R. E. Welsh, *In Relief of Doubt*, pp. 23-24.

[25]*Ibid.*, pp. 210-22.

XII.   PROCRASTINATION MAY HARDEN THE HEART

The person who continually hears a truth and is exhorted to obey it, but for various reasons postpones until a convenient season his obedience to that truth, gradually becomes hardened to it until finally it may lose its appeal to him. His constant refusal to obey the truth, his continual crushing of his better impulses which call on him to obey it, harden his heart. It may finally become so hardened that it doubts and denies the truth, perhaps in an effort to justify its disobedience. He who refuses to walk in the light has invited the darkness and the longer he continues in the darkness the farther he gets from the light and the more difficult it will be for him to find the light. Much precedes this individual's final rejection of Christ. As Dr. Lamont wrote: "Many steps have preceded the final rejection. Every step in the fatal descent has meant the man's expenditure of the potential freedom which is his birthright. It has therefore meant increasing bondage. This is the inevitable corollary to the rejection of the overtures of the Divine Spirit who has kept knocking at his door. Now, it is God who is the author and substainer of the moral order. It is he who has ordained that the man who perserves along the right road will become a better man, while he who persists in keeping to the wrong road will become a worse man. If a person commits a sin without repenting he is thereby changed for the worse. Were this not so, there would be no moral order at all. And if the person continues in his downward career a climax is bound to be reached. To defy the light is to court darkness, and the time may come in the dismal process when the last beam of God's light has departed from the soul.[26]

XIII.   UNWILLINGNESS TO SUBMIT TO ITS HIGH MORAL STANDARD

Wordsworth spoke of a "revolt from the severe claims of religion and a secret inclination to sin which dwells in many hearts. Such an explanation of unbelief is one from which charity and courtesy alike would shrink, and it often seems obviously

---

[26]Dr. Daniel Lamont, *The Anchorage of Life,* London: The Inter-Varsity Fellowship, 39 Bedford Square, W. C. 1, 1940, p. 140.

inapplicable; but a serious testing of what religion is and of the very heavy strain which it puts upon the believer, must convince us that the difficulty is no imaginary one. For experience shows us that no amount of intellect, or high culture, of noble ambition, can save a man from grave moral faults; and that even apparently sincere conviction sometimes breaks down, in cases of men who seem entirely raised above temptation. No one, I believe, can really know his own heart, without knowing also that he is by nature capable of almost any sin, and that there is within him a constant pressure, sometimes gentle, sometimes vehement, tending to make light of the responsibility for sin, and to weaken belief in the justice and love of God." All of us know how easy it is for an individual to rationalize and to excuse himself from any heavy responsibility for his own conduct. It is easy for an indivi- dual, as he thinks about the sinful things that he would like to do; as he meditates on the pleasures of sin; as he does things that are wrong; to feel more and more that these things are not so bad after all; and that therefore the book, the Bible, which sets them forth in such a terrible light cannot be right. "This pressure," continued Wordsworth, "if once we yield to it, tends directly to unbelief in revelation; for the moral conscience longs above all things to slumber, and in the full brightness, all hope of peaceful repose in sin is lost; and therefore he whose heart inclines to sin, instinctively veils himself from the knowledge of revelation, just as the sick man tosses uneasily until the stream of sunlight is curtained from his pillow."[27]

H. G. Wells, one of the most publicized unbelievers of our day has borne striking testimony to this cause of unbelief. It shows that he himself recognized that one of the reasons that people have not accepted Christianity is that it brings their deeds to the light and shows them how sinful and small they are in much of their conduct. And remember that he was an avowed unbeliever. In fact, the writer heard him say, outside the Opera House in San Francisco, California just before America entered the war, that he was an atheist. Here is his statement concerning Jesus. "He was too great for his disciples. And in view of what

---

[27]*The One Religion*, p. 13.

he plainly said, is it any wonder that all who were rich and pros-perous felt a horror of strange things, a swimming of their world at his teaching. Perhaps the priests and the rulers and the rich men understood him better than his followers. He was dragging out all the little private reservations they had made from social service into the light of a universal religous life. He was like some terrible moral huntsman digging mankind out of the snug burrows in which they had lived hitherto. In the white blaze of this kingdom of his there was to be no property. (Wells is wrong about this; although Christ did teach that man was a steward and not, in one sense, the actual owner, and then it is required of stewards that they be found faithful, J. D. B.), no privilege, no pride and precedence; no motive indeed and no reward by love. Is it any wonder that men were dazzled and blinded and cried out against him. Even his disciples cried out when he would not spare them the light. Is it any wonder that the priests realized that between this man and themselves there was no choice but that he or priestcraft should perish? Is it any wonder that the Roman soldiers, confronted and amazed by something soaring over their comprehension and threatening all their discipline, should take refuge in wild laughter, and crown him with thorns and robe him in purple and make a mock Caesar of him? For to take him seriously was to enter upon a strange and alarming life, to abandon habits, to control instincts and impulses, to essay an incredible happiness. . . .

"Is it any wonder that to this day this Galilean is too much for our small hearts." (H. G. Wells, *The Outline of History*, 4th Edition, Vol. II:598-599 (New York: The Review of Reviews Company, 1924.)

H. G. Wells recognized that men would turn against Jesus, and that they would in various ways deny and oppose his message, because it made such tremendous demands on life. And thus some unbelief is simply a rationalization for what is really a desire to escape from the tremendous ethical demands made by Christ on believers. In order to escape from the demands of that Teacher and message individuals sometimes flee from faith: for if they believed they would feel under an obligation to live in harmony with the message. To live with an easy conscience, and at the same time to live on a much lower level than that established by Jesus, men have denied His authority and claims. And certainly this must be a potent cause of unbelief when even such an eminent unbeliever as Wells recognized it.

If an individual replies that this cannot be a cause of unbelief because there are unbelievers who do not go into immorality when they depart from the faith, our answer is severalfold. *First,* men are sometimes glad to get away from the moral authority of the Christian faith not because they want to do some things that it forbids, but because some of the things which it sanctions and commands they do not want to do. *Second,* the sinful attitude of heart may not be of the type that we generally associate with immorality, but such as the pride of individuals who do not want to admit that they are a long way from what they ought to be. Such an individual may welcome unbelief because it removes from his sight the accusing high standard of the Christian faith which passes judgement on his life which is willing to remain on a lower level of both positive and negative morality. *Third,* the collapse in moral conduct may not come immediately because, as we have elsewhere pointed out, the habits of the individual, and his attitudes, have been constructed by Christian morality and he finds it difficult to break away from them and to get over the idea of the shamefulness of certain types of conduct. As Wordsworth pointed out, these sinful inclinations may be deep in the heart of an individual and may not immediately manifest themselves in sinful conduct. "This is the interior state; outside, for a time there is perhaps no apparent change. The force of sinful inclinations appears to have spent itself in producing unbelief. The force of habit still remains to balance it. An equilibrium seems to be produced in the man, and no striking and glaring evil marks the moment of lapse into infidelity. It seems almost as if the state of unbelief were not such a bad one after all, and death may intervene before the strife of powers has been decided within the soul. But often even to our eyes, there comes a sudden collapse, and the apparent peace which preceded it is found to have been merely a quiet rottenness." (The One Religion, pp. 13-14). *Fourth,* it has not been suggested that this is the only cause of unbelief.

XV. The Right Mind-Set Is Necessary

It was this truth, this challenge, and this warning, that Jesus placed before mankind when he said: "If any man willeth to do his will, he shall know of the teaching whether it is of God, or whether I speak from myself." (John 7:17). Much of the teaching of Jesus deals with the life that now is and the way it is to be lived. Since Christianity is the way of life, it is evident that its full claim; its full power; and its full credentials cannot be tested apart from life itself. Christianity deals with the whole man, not with merely his intellect, but also his heart, his will, and his conduct. Thus it cannot be completely tested apart from the supreme test of life; the test of conduct and what it does to, in, and for, life. The Bible Commentary commented as follows on this verse: "If it be any man's will to do His will. The force of the argument lies in the moral harmony of the man's purpose with the divine law so far as this law is known or felt. If there be no sympathy there can be no understanding. Religion is a matter of life and not of thought only."

Professor Meyer shows how that this verse not only relates one's conduct with the test of Christianity, but shows how that one's desire to do what is true, to follow the will of God, is also involved. This verse offers therefore not merely a test of the truth of Christianity, but also the test of what is in man's heart. It does not mean, of course, that one may know at first all that God has required, but that one must have honesty of heart and love of truth so that he wants above all else to do the will of God when he can find that will. *"The condition of knowing this is that one be willing*—have it as the moral aim of his self-determination—*to do the will of God.* He who is wanting in this, who lacks fundamentally the moral determination of his mind towards God, and to whom, therefore, Christ's teaching is something strange, for the recognition of which as divine there is in the ungodly bias of his will no point of contact or of sympathy; this knowledge is to him a moral impossibility. On the contrary, the bias towards the fulfilling of God's will is the subjective factor necessary to the recognition of divine doctrine as such; for this doctrine produces the immediate conviction that it is certainly divine by virtue of the moral likeness and sympathy of its nature with the man's own nature. (Compare Aristotle, Ethics ix. 3,iii.1). Accordingly, we certainly have in this passage the *testimonium internum,* but not in the ordinary theological sense, as a thing for those who already believe, but for those who do not yet believe, and to whom the divine teaching of the Lord presents itself for the first time. . . .(it) however, must not be limited either to a definite *form of the revelation* of it (the will of God), to any one particular *requirement* (that of faith in Christ), which would contradict the fact that the axiom is stated without any limitation; it must be taken in its full breadth and com-prehensiveness—'that which God wills,' whatever, how, and wherever this will may require. Also the natural moral law within (Rom. 1:20 ff., ii.14,15) is not excluded, though those who heard the words spoken must have referred the general statement to the revelation given to *them* in the law and the prophets."[28] This as has been observed, does not mean that one must believe without any evidence, but that one must have a *disposition* which is willing to do God's will. And even the rank unbeliever, if he will stop and think a moment, will acknowledge that if God is and if He has revealed His will to mankind that man-kind ought to obey that will. The willingness to do this is the disposition, the condition of heart, which is necessary. This dis-position will find that the Word itself is one of its own witnesses. To such a condition of heart it commends itself. And, as pointed out in the appendix in the extended quotations from Dr. Butler, this disposition of heart will not rest as long as there is any indica-tion of evidence which can be examined and which seems to promise to lead one to the will of God. On the other hand, we can readily see how the individual who has his heart set against God, who would be unwilling to do God's will even if he saw it, is not likely to see the evidence that Christianity is from God. In

---

[28]Dr. Heinrich August Wilhelm Meyer, *Critical and Exergetical Hand-Book,* New York: Funk and Wagnalls, 1884, pp. 236-237.

rebellion to God, he is not apt to seek out the evidence which emphasizes his condemned condition and will tend to make him uncomfortable and unsettled in his rebellion.

SOME BOOKS WHICH ARE RECOMMENDED

While on the subject of reading in Christian evidence, it will be well to mention some books on the subject. There are literally thousands of books on the subject of Christian evidence. The author in his own personal library, has over a thousand volumes on the subject. Out of such a large number of volumes it is difficult to select a few which will appeal in the same degree to all different types of mind. The following are not the only books, nor necessarily the best, but they are good books. Dr. Leander S. Keyser, A System of Christian Evidences (Burlington, Iowa: The Lutheran Literary Board, 1942) has a list of some books on different phases of Christian Evidence (pp. 259-283)

Nelson, Byron C. *After Its Own Kind,* The Augsburg Publishing Co., Minneapolis, Minn.

Evolution, (I. C. C. 366 Bay St., Toronto 1, Ontario, Canada.)

Christlieb T., *Modern Doubt and Christian Belief* (Out of print. Sometimes found in second-hand book stores.)

McGarvery, J. W., *Evidences of Christianity.* Also *Biblical Criticism* (Cincinnati, Ohio: Standard Publishing Company).

Nelson, David, *The Cause and Cure of Infidelity* (New York: George H. Doran Company).

Machen, J. G., *The Origin of Paul's Religion.* Also *The Virgin Birth* (Grand Rapids, Mich.: Eerdman's Publishing Co.) This Company has recently republished several of his books on evidence.

Price, G. M., Q. E. D.: *New Light on the Doctrine of Creation.* Other books also which can be secured from the Pacific Publishing Association, Mountain View, Calif.

Hamilton, Floyd E., *The Basis of Christian Faith* (New York: Harper and Brothers). Very good.

Smith, Wilbur M., *Therefore Stand,* (Boston, Mass,: W. A. Wilde Co.)

Paley, William, *Evidences of Christianity.* Found in second-hand book stores.

Fawthrop, T. W., *The Stones Cry Out* (London: Marshall, Morgan and Scott, Ltd).

W. H. Turton, *The Truth of Christianity.*

Hammond, T. C., *Reasoning Faith* (London: The Inter-Varsity Fellowship, 39 Bedford Square, London W. C. 1.)

The Victoria Institute (12, Queen Anne's Gate, London, England). Their various pamphlets and volumes of transactions. Material published by the Evolution Protest Movement may also be secured from them.

Short, A. Rendle, *Modern Discovery and the Bible* (London: The Inter-Varsity Fellowship, 39 Bedford Square, London, W. C. 1).

Bales, James D., Editor, *The Thinking Christian* (Quarterly journal devoted to the Bible and modern thought. $1.50 per year.)

Clark, Robert E. D., Editor, *Science and Religion* (Quarterly journal. $1.50 per year. Paternoster Press, Ludgate House, Fleet St., London, E. C. 4, England.)

Some of the above mentioned foreign publications are handled by Inter-Varsity Christian Fellowship, 64 E. Lake St., Chicago, Ill. and 30 St. Mary St., Toronto 5, Ontario. Send for their catalog.

CHAPTER V

CHRISTIAN FAITH IS NOT CREDULITY

Believing that Christian faith is credulity, mere blind super-stition, many unbelievers scoffingly turn aside from Christianity. Why should we close our eyes to facts, to evidence, they reason; and since, they assume, Christianity calls on us to do this we can-not accept Christianity. This misconception of the nature of Christian faith may be due to a number of factors: such as a prejudice on the part of the unbeliever that will not admit that Christianity has any evidence on which to stand; to an unfair treatment of the Bible wherein passages, which condemn as im-moral certain forms of unbelief, are taken out of their context; to an indifference to those passages which clearly teach that faith is based on facts, and to a misconception of Christian faith which is presented by some ignorant believers; ignorant, that is, of the Bible teaching concerning the basis of faith.

I. There Are Two Kinds of Doubts

Failing to distinguish between things that are different, un-believers conclude that any form of doubt is automatically con-demned by the Scriptures. There is doubt which is due to a failure to understand an argument or to see certain facts because these facts have not yet been presented to the individual. On the other hand, there is a doubt which is due to a refusal to listen to an argument and a rejection of facts. "The critical attitude may come from a genuine desire to know the truth or it may come from a desire to avoid unpleasant truth. In the one case it is not sinful, in the other it is a sin against the light and is therefore one of the worst sins. But outwardly the two things appear very much the same, though many think that they are capable of detecting 'arguing for the sake of arguing'."[1]

---

[1] Robert E. D. Clark, *Conscious and Unconscious Sin*, pp. 43-44.

The Bible does not condemn the attitude which is unwilling to believe without evidence. Christians are warned not to believe every prophet; to try those who profess to be apostles; to beware of false teachers and to detect their falsehood by their fruits (Matt. 7: 15-18; 1 John 4: 1-2; Rev. 2:2). Prove all things, hold fast that which is good, is the apostolic adominition (1 Thess. 5:21). The doubt of Thomas and the doubt of John's disciples was dealt with without harshness, but with the presentation of proof which took away the basis for doubt (John 20:24-30).

Doubt, however, was condemned when it was due to a refusal to see the truth and to a carnal condition of heart which the possessor was determined to maintain. "How can ye believe," said Jesus, "who receive glory one of another, and the glory that cometh from the only God ye seek not? Think not that I will accuse you to the Father: there is one that accuseth you, even Moses, on whom ye have set your hope. For if ye believed Moses, ye would believe me; for he wrote of me. But if ye believe not his writings, how shall ye believe my words?" (John 5:44-47). In the same context He said: "But I know you, that ye have not the love of God in yourselves." (John 5:42).

II. FAITH IS NOT CREDULITY

One of the convincing proofs that the New Testament does not call for credulity is that the type of mind, which it maintains is necessary for faith, is the very type which any scientist would say is necessary in order to discover and accept truth. Some of these characteristics are: (1) Humility (Matt. 18:1-4). (2) Love the truth (John 18:37; 8:32). (3) Willing to hear (Rom. 10:17). (4) Willing to prove things (1 Thess. 5:21). (5) Refuse to be shackled by passions and thus to always believe only what pleases (2 Tim. 4:3-4; 2 Thess. 2:10-12). (6) Refuse to accept, without testing, everyone and just anything (1 John 4:1; Rev.2:2). (7) Have a good and honest heart (Lk. 8:15). What better attitude of heart and mind can any person have than to have the one recommended by the Bible? How can any but the credulous, or the uninformed, believe that the Bible recommends credulity?

III. The Childlike Heart

One of the passages which is used to prove that Christianity recommends credulity is found in Matt. 18:1-3. A brief glance at it, however, should enable a person to see that Jesus is not recommending every characteristic of childhood but one which the disciples sorely needed and which scientist recognize as essential to learning, i.e. humility and a willingness to be taught. "In that hour came the disciples unto Jesus saying Who then is greatest in the kingdom of heaven? And he called to him a little child, and set him in the midst of them, and said, Verily I say unto you, Except ye turn and become as little children, ye shall in no wise enter into the kingdom of heaven. Whosoever *therefore shall humble* himself as this little child, the same is the greatest in the kingdom of heaven." The person who is not humble will not admit his ignorance and thus his need for instruction. And thus he will not hear and examine the truth which is presented to him, especially those truths which may strike a blow at his intellectual and spiritual pride.

An excellent extensive treatment of this statement of Jesus will be found in Richard Whately's *Essays on Some of the Peculiarities of the Christian Faith*. The reader will be impressed not only with the fact that Jesus did not commend credulity in this passage, but that this passage is one of the indications of the wisdom of Jesus.

To this subject of the childlike heart and of the true nature of Christian faith it is our intention to return, the Lord willing, in a book on *Faith and Facts*. In this we shall abundantly establish that *faith is based on facts; that faith legitimately goes beyond the immediate facts;* and that *faith also leads to facts.*

IV. False Conception of Doubt Is a Cause of Apostasy

Some believers who have been taught that all doubt is evil, and that it should be crushed out of their minds, may not always be able to dispel it. These doubts, because they are taught that they are evil in themselves, are not brought to the light, solved, and followed by an increase of faith. Instead, they are crowded into the back of the mind and there they lurk and from time to

time are joined by other doubts which the individual is endeavoring to crush. These are not really forgotten and as they increase
in number they tend to build up a certain bias or prejudice in
the mind which tends to take the heart and peace out of their
religion and may finally result in unbelief. Dr. Clark has well
analyzed this type of treatment of doubt. "If conscience suggests
that certain rationalist arguments ought to be examined, there
can be no excuse for suppressing it. After all, when this happens,
doubt is *already* present and it is honesty, not sin, to admit the
fact. Furthermore, if doubts are not admitted, they wll accumu-
late in the subconscious mind in an undigested form where they
are bound to influence behaviour, where they produce hypocrisy
and where in many cases they burst forth and cause an apparently
keen Christian to reverse his moral character. The fact that
suppressed doubt is doubt nevertheless, and is very dangerous
psychologically, constitutes another strong reason why conscience
must never be suppressed on the ground that it appears to be
evil. Clearly, it is far better to know that one doubts than to
remain outwardly an enthusiastic Christian and know that if
the Bible means what it says, Christ will ultimately make public
the secrets of all hearts, and expose our unbelief. These are the
secrets which need exposing now.

"Every doubt, as with all other promptings of conscience,
must be faced as it comes. Sometimes the answers may not be
found at once, but the questions raised must often be allowed
to enter the field of consciousness so that a look-out may always
be kept for resolutions. But, generaly speaking, sufficent unto
the day is the evil thereof, provided the evil of many days is
not crowded into one.

"It is here, however, that there is danger. It often happens
that a Christian represses his doubts for a long time, and then
decides to face up to them of a sudden. In such a case arguments against his faith have collected at the back of the mind,
while their answers have not so collected. Hence, when the
doubts are admitted, the position is hopelessly one-sided, and it
often leads to an abandonment of faith. The life histories of many
agnostics who were formerly professed Christians show that

the change was produced in this way. Unfortunately, in such a moment of crisis, the bias to which the judgment is subjected may be lost sight of. It would seem best, therefore, that the transition from a dishonest to an honest attitude towards doubts should be brought about very slowly, or if this is impossible that the probable psychological result of what is in effect a study of only one side of the problem, should be kept strongly in mind."[2] That is, the individual should not try to face all of his doubts at once. They have not accumulated all at once and they cannot be solved all at once (especially when a bias has already been built up in the mind by the mass of unsolved difficulties) since this means an attempt to solve some particular difficulty in an atmosphere of doubt. Then, too, as pointed out in the section on viewing the evidence before concentrating on the difficulties, one cannot get a proper view of either the evidence or the objec- tions unless he does make the right type of approach.

It is clear that one should seek the solution of difficulties instead of trying to hide them from oneself. In many cases, to state clearly the difficulty may be enough to enable one to see that it offers no real problem to faith. Then, too, since one knows the exact difficulty he can keep his eyes open for material which will solve it. One will not, of course, take time off in every case until he finds the solution, for the answer may not turn up for some time. It may come when one is reading or thinking on some other subject. Thus one may lay aside a prob- lem for a time, but since he has faced it squarely in the beginning he can always be on the lookout for light on it. In the meantime he goes about his daily life without any undue disturbance of mind, for he has avoided the anxiety of mind, and the building up of a bias against faith, which often comes when one sup- presses his problems in an effort to keep from admitting to him- self that he has had some problems presented to him.

V. Credulity Is Condemned

Of the idea that faith is not connected with evidence Dr. Whately wrote as follows: "The faith which the Christian Scrip-

---

[2]*Conscious and Unconscious Sin,* pp. 39-40.

tures speak of and command, is the very contrary of that blind sort of belief and trust which does not rest on any good reason. This last is more properly called *credulity* than faith. When a man believes without evidence, or against evidence, he is what we rightly called credulous. But he is never commended for this; on the contrary, we often find in Scripture mention made of persons who are reproached for their unbelief or want of faith, precisely on account of their showing this kind of credulity; that is, not judging fairly according to the evidence, but resolving to believe only what was agreeable to their prejudices, and to trust any one who flattered those prejudices."

When the sacred writers "commend a man's faith, it is because he listens fairly to evidence, and judges according to the reasons laid before him. The difficulty and the virtue of faith consists in a man's believing and trusting, not against *evidence,* but against his expectations and prejudices, against his inclinations, and passion, and interests. We read, accordingly, that Jesus offered sufficient proof of his coming from God. . ." Although He manifested His power in signs and wonders they attributed it to the power of the devil and otherwise brought objections against Christ.

"But if He had come among them offering to fulfill their expectations, and undertaking to deliver their country from the Romans ,then even though He had shown no miraculous power, many of them would have received Him readily. And indeed it is recorded of Him, that He declared this himself, and foretold to his disciples, 'Many will come in my name,' (that is, taking on them my character,) 'saying, I am (the) Christ, and will deceive many.' And again 'I am come in my Father's name,' (that is, with my Father's authority and power) 'and you receive me not; if another shall come in his own name,' (that is, requiring to be believed on his bare word, without any miraculous signs,) 'him ye will receive.'

"And so it came to pass: for in the last siege of Jerusalem many impostors came forward, each one claiming to be the Christ, and drawing mutitudes to follow him, and leading them to make the most desperate resistance to the Romans: till at length the city was taken and the nation utterly overthrown.

"Now the Jews who believed any one of these impostors were led to do so by their prejudices, and expectations, and wishes not by any proof that was offered. They showed, therefore, more credulity than the Christians did. And these unbelieving Jews, as they are called, are the very persons who were reproached for their want of faith. You may plainly see from this, that the faith which the Christian writers speak of is not blind credulity, but fairness in listening to evidence, and judging accordingly, without being led away by prejudices and inclinations."[3]

It is thus clear that all forms of doubt are not considered, in the Bible, as sinful in themselves. One should not, however, conclude that because Christ did not condemn all forms of doubt, that doubt is to be regarded as an end in itself. One should deal with his doubts, but he should not deliberately seek to raise them just for the purpose of toying with them and for an intellectual thrill in solving them. Neither should one cultivate the attitude of mind which wants to stand off in a critical attitude which prides itself on its refusal to render a decision and make commitments. The passions of man are too ready to encourage us in deceptive rationalizations for one to play or toy with doubt (See Clark, Conscious and Unconscious Sin, p. 44.)

VI. The New Testament Teaches That Faith Is Based on Evidence

The way in which the New Testament appeals for faith proves that it does not ask people to believe without evidence or contrary to the evidence. In the Gospel of John the appeal is made to miracles (John 2:11; 2:23; 3:2; 20:30); works (5:35); the Father's witness (5:36,37); the witness of Moses and of the Scriptures (5:39-47); and the self-evidencing power of the truth (John 7:17). In the book of Acts in one sermon appeal is made to the evidence of prophecy (2:6, 23, 30-31, 34); miracles of Christ (2:22); the resurrection (2:27-32); and the miraculous

---

[3]Richard Whately, *Introductory Lessons on Morals, and Christian Evidences*, Cambridge: 1856, pp. 196-199.

demonstrations then taking place (2:33). It is possible for men
to ignore or reject the New Testament record and assert that
these things are not reliable, but it is impossible for any informed
student to be honest and say that by faith the New Testament
means credulity.

VII. THE UNBELIEF WHICH IS SINFUL IN ITSELF

The passages enable us to understand how one kind of
doubt and unbelief is sinful of itself, since it involves a rejection
of or a refusal to give heed to evidence. Jesus taught that there
is doubt which is sinful in itself, for He stated that the Spirit
would reprove, or convict the world of sin "because they believe
in me." (John 16:8-9). "Now, before any of you shrink back
from the supposed harshness of these words of Christ consider
the value, the admitted value, of the principle on which they
rest; and consider also that its establishment is due to Christianity.
You will all agree that neglect of truth that it is in your power
to obtain (and which is vital to life, J. D. B.) is sinful, and sinful in proportion to the value of the subject matter.   This extension of the field of duty so as to include the field of knowledge,
is one of the triumphs of Christian moral philosophy, to which
modern scientific advance owes more than it is likely to confess.
Aristotle said, 'All men naturally desire to know;' our Lord
said, in fact, 'It is the duty of all men to know,' and especially
to know the highest of all truths, that of religion. If it is culpable
for a young man to be ignorant of some book which he offers
for examination; if it is more sinful for us who teach here to
be ignorant of the subjects which we profess; if it is wrong to be
ignorant of the laws of health; and, worse still, to be ignorant of
the moral laws which bind man to man: how much more sinful
than all is it to be ignorant of our relations to God! Supposing
that truth respecting religion is within our reach, and as long
as the least hope of obtaining it glimmers before us, we are com-
mitting a very grievous sin indeed in resting contented in ignorance. For by so doing we neglect the highest perfection of which
we are capable; we distinctly determine to be worse than we have
the power of being, less vigorous in our motives, less definite in

our hopes of the future, less noble in our aspirations for ourselves and our fellow-men. For we determine to know less and think less of God, from whom all goodness flows, and in whom all hope of joy centers."[4] Those who are content with unbelief without making a serious, fair, examination of the credentials of Christ have by that very attitude judged themselves to be of a very worldly nature and uninterested in spiritual, eternal things.

Those who think that there is no guilt in rejecting historical facts, such as those which show, among other lines of evidence, that Jesus is the Christ, seem to be blind to the fact that "most principles which men reject or accept can be viewed as historic facts, past, present, or future, or one, or all. Most principles which men accept or reject are, however apparently abstract, probably found only in some historic concrete. The wickedness of an assassination, a treason, a robbery, is a historical fact; and yet the perpetrators are bound to recognize and accept the truth, and obey the obligation that truth imposes.

"God is a historical fact through eternal ages. His existence, his administration, his incarnation, are all historic facts which only need in like manner to be properly authenticated to impose a corresponding obligation. The truth of Christ's divine mission clearly authenticates itself as other facts of history although it may impose obligations as much more imperative as it is a more stupendous fact; its rejection may aggravate guilt in the degree of the importance of its prevalence over the world; and that same rejection inexcusable in its nature, may produce ruin as a natural consequence of its rejecting the Redeemer and his redemption. And if the aggravation of the guilt of that rejection be proportioned to the importance of the prevalence of that religion, and that religion be for the redemption of the world from ruin, then does it follow, as by an involution, that the guilt of that rejection deserves the ruin in which it tends to involve the world.

"If a man be responsible for the guilty use of his hand, is he not responsible for a misuse of his brain?" And, after all, is

---

[4]John Wordsworth, *The One Religion,* London: Longmans, Green and Co., 1893, pp. 6-7.

not the hand used as an instrument of unrighteousness only because the brain and heart have thought unrighteous thoughts;
planned unrighteous deeds; and called on the hand to carry out
those plans? "If the unholy use of the eye be guilty, is not
the dishonest use of the intellect? Are all our powers responsible
save our truth-seeking faculty? And how know we that God
has never propounded a *test-truth* to probationary men, by the
acceptance or reception of which the honesty of each mans truth-
seeking faculty is infallibily decided? When such a *test-fact*
is presented, the act of rejection reveals the reprobate, decides his
moral ruin, and works a series of disastrous and responsible consequences. Such a *test-fact* the divine Incarnate does announce
himself to be, and surely no more suitable *test-fact* in the universe
can exist. *For a discrimination am I come into the world, that
they which see not* the truth they seek *might see it: and that
they which see* with a truth-avoiding spirit *might be made,* in
fact, what they are in purpose, blind. John 9:39. Under that
assumption, his rejecters are by himself and his apostles, throughout the New Testament, placed under the ban of moral condemnation. Rejection of him is the parent sin which produces all other
sins, and prevents their expiation or pardon. 'He that believeth
not shall be damned. Some are led *away by the error of the
wicked.* There is a *deceivableness of unrighteousness.* There are
those who *deny the Lord that bought* them. In fine, 'There is
a way that *seemeth right* to a man, but the end thereof is death.'
Nor do the New Testament writers ostentatiously display their
friendship for the deniers of the great *Test.* Neither St. Peter,
St. Jude, nor St. John speaks blandly of them. They know no
innocent unbelievers, no excusable infidels. In fine, pleasant as
the sunny theology may seem, which holds anti-christian doctrine
to be the venial error of a man as honest and as well off as believers, it has no authority in Scripture nor in reason. There is
a solemn, awful side to God's word; a dark and terrible phase
in God's moral system, at which it becomes us to tremble; nor
can we ignore it wisely, any more than we can ignore the tragic
depths of woe that lie entombed in the whole groaning creation
that travaileth until now.

"Are there such sins as sins of *the Spirit,* in contradistinction to sins of *the flesh?* Is there any responsibility for the use or misuse of our intellectual powers? A murderer, a traitor, is guilty of sin, sin of the flesh. . .But what shall we say of the intellectualist that promulgates the sophism that led the murderer to the murder, and the traitor to his treason? The gross, external, muscular sinner is thus cruelly damned; while the refined, internal, cerebral sinner, though really the primely responsible, is glorified. Are we, then accountable only for the deeds of our hands, and not for the exercise of our brains? And all this resolves itself into the one great question, a question which the transiently great men of our day would do well to ponder—*Are we in any way responsible for our moral beliefs?*"

Has the unbeliever, regardless of how he may have performed some of his duties toward his fellowman, performed his duty to God? And if one has not performed his duty to God, and endeavored to get other men to do likewise, he has not performed his full duty to man. "Was reverence to the divine in his heart, prayer to the Supreme upon his lips, communion with the Holy Spirit in his spirit? Who was it that said, 'Thou shalt *love* the Lord thy God with all thy heart'. . . . Is it true, or is it not, that God is the great good; indifference to God the great apostasy; separation from God the great damnation? If these are truths they cannot be sacrificed in compliment to the good behavior of Henry Wright. They are not to be judged by Henry Wright; they it is that must judge Henry Wright. What right has any man to suppress all the high and holy intuitions that God has bestowed upon him, to exclude the aspirations of the spirit toward the divine Spirit; to cast off fear and restrain prayer; to give heed only to those lower faculties that tell of matter and its properties, and then come forth to the world and proclaim that God does not exist? It *was* this suppression that made Mr. Wright the 'fool'. It was an evil heart of unbelief.' And we do class all 'skepticism' that rejects God as revealed to us 'as a certain mark of sinful folly.' Atheism is in itself a heinous sin. It is not a *crime* which man may punish, but a *sin* which God will judge. And the apostle

truly and justly pronounces a final judgment upon "those that
know not God, and obey not the Gospel of his Son."[5]

VIII. The Seeker Must Love the Truth

Paul spoke of those who "received not *the love of the truth*,
that they might be saved. And for this cause God sendeth them
a working of error, that they should believe a lie: that they all
might be judged who believed not the truth but had *pleasure in
unrighteousness*.' (Thess. 2:10-12). They do not love truth therefore they are not attracted to it and even when they see it they
hastily reject it and rationalize their reaction. When the truth
about themselves is unpleasant they become offended and seek
for the pleasant thing, even if it has to be a deceitful thing in
order to be pleasant. They are like those who have "itching ears,
will heap to themselves teachers after their own lusts; and will
turn away their ears from the truth, and turn aside unto fables."
(2 Tim. 4:3-4). They also refuse to listen to the truth when it
condemns the unrighteous things in which they find pleasure and
which they are determined to continue. Thus they seek for some
message which will assure them that the unrighteous thing is
right and thus permit them to continue in it without being re-
buked by their conscience. And thus it happens to them as it
happened to some of the old of whom God said: "Behold, I will
bring evil upon this people, even the fruit of their thoughts, because they have not hearkened unto my words; and as for my
law, they have rejected it." (Jer. 6:19). God sends such people
strong delusions in that He has ordained the laws of man's heart
and of morality, and that person who has no love for the truth
and who lives in and takes pleasure in unrighteousness will unfit
his heart for the reception of truth and fit it for the reception of
strong delusions which comfort and assure him in his error and
unrighteousness; error and unrighteousness which he is determined
to maintain.

---

[5]Dr. Daniel D. Whedon, *Statements: Theological and Critical*, New
York: Phillips and Hunt, 1887, pp. 168-170, 172-173.

CHAPTER VI

THE MORAL NATURE OF FAITH

The fact that one must love the truth indicates that the attitude of heart has something to do with whether or not one will believe. This was also brought out in the parable of the sower. Moral qualities, and not merely external evidence, are involved. The person who does not love the truth, and who takes pleasure in unrighteousness, will not be very willing to receive the message which emphasizes love for the truth, and which strongly condemns unrighteousness. The person who is unwilling seriously to consider the meaning and destiny of life, the person who lightly throws away his marvelous moral and spiritual capacities, this person will not find himself in a frame of mind to weigh the evidence for the message which holds life to be the most serious trust which has ever been committed to man. He who wants a careless, immoral life, will not want the faith which is a constant rebuke to such a life. Those, however, who hunger and thirst after righteousness will be filled for they not only fairly examine the evidence, but they will see in the Christian faith the answer to the deeper needs of the human soul.[1]

I. SAVING FAITH IS VOLUNTARY

"Saving faith is voluntary. Had the revelation been so strong that anyone beholding it could not disbelieve, any more than he could dissent from a mathematical demonstration, that would have been no recommendation; for it would have overridden

---

[1] Bishop Butler, in his famous *Analogy*, has emphasized that even the difficulties involved in believing are just those difficulties which bring out what is really in us and what we really want to continue to do in life. Because he has something important to say on this subject, the author is reprinting in the appendix some material from his pen. Admittedly it is difficult reading at times, but who wants easy reading all of the time? Concentrate on it, stop and think about what you have read, and you will find it most stimulating. Without endorsing every word in it, it is commended to you for your consideration.

moral freedom, and would have been a kind of evidence unsuitable to moral subjects. That it is possible for a man, by diverting his attention, by wilfully perverting his judgment, by sinister misapprehension, by disingenuous examination, by giving exclusive welcome to agreeable fallacies, or by culpable ignorance to refuse both the salvation and the light which reveals it, and also possible, by an opposite treatment, to realize the opposite result, corresponds with the moral nature to which revelation appeals, and which makes the individual the arbiter of his own character and destiny. 'There is light enough for those whose sincere wish is to see, and darkness enough to confound those of an opposite disposition.' (Pascal). The most central and impressive of all revelations was the word of Jesus Christ; but that was moral and resistible, for many who heard it 'were offended.' In like manner, resistance and disbelief of His written message is no proof of its insufficiency."[2]

II. The Nature of the Evidence Brings Out What Is in a Person

"Whereas, may it not be said, that irresistible evidence would confound all characters and all dispositions? Would subvert, rather than promote, the true purpose of the divine counsels; which is, not to produce *obedience* by a force little short of mechanical constraint, (which obedience would be regularity, not virtue, and would hardly perhaps differ from that which inanimate bodies pay to the laws impressed upon their nature,) but to treat moral agents agreeably to what they are: which is done, when light and motives are of such kinds, and are imparted in such measure, *that influence on them depends upon the recipients themselves?*"[3]

III. Faith May Be Blocked by Pride

The quotation from Dr. Micklen is an excellent illustration of the fact that the gospel does bring out what is in a man. If man

---

[2]Marshall Randles, *The Design and Use of Holy Scripture*, London: Wesleyan Methodist Book Room, 1893, pp. 32-33.

[3]William Paley, *Evidences of Christianity*, Cambridge: University Press, 1849, p. 285.

does not want the truth, if he holds something else more precious than the truth, that man will not believe the gospel, and the cause of his unbelief reveals that the trouble is with man and not with the gospel. The gospel is too great a blow to man's pride for some to accept it. "The Christian gospel is this, that when man by searching could not find God, and when man by striving could not find peace, and when human life was like an agonized question to the sullen, lowering heavens, then God spoke. More, in our extremity and desperate need, he came himself. The majesty of God took the form of a Servant. The Word was made flesh and dwelt among us; he was crucified for our sins, and rose for our justification. That is the mystery of the incarnation.

> O loving wisdom of our God!
> When all was sin and shame,
> A second Adam to the fight,
> And to the rescue came.

'When all was sin and shame'—that is the crux! It is the recognition of a sore wound at the heart of humanity, which no earthly balm could ever stanch; it implies that all men, even the emancipated and the cultivated, are lost without a Savior, and that redemption is not to be achieved by our fumbling efforts and our ineffectual regret. The ultimate scandal of evangelical religion (which in this connection includes both historic Protestantism and the Church of Rome but excludes much of modern Protestantism) lies not in dogma or symbolism but in its intolerable offense to human pride.

> Nothing in my hand I bring;
> Simply to thy cross I cling—

It is that which the man of taste and culture cannot bring himself to say; he feels no need of so utter a salvation; to him therefore it is nonsense or mere mythology that the majesty of God should take a Servant's form."[4]

---

[4]Dr. Nathaniel Micklem, "On the Aversion of Men of Taste to Evangelical Religion," *Christendom,* Vol. I, Autumn, 1936, No. 5, p. 761.

IV. One Must Examine Himself As Well As the Evidence

Those who overlook the moral nature of faith are apt to conclude quickly that the reason they do not believe in Christ is due to a lack of evidence, or because the evidence, in other words, does not meet a standard which they in their own minds have determined that it must meet if they are to believe. They ought to ask themselves several searching questions. *First,* have I really weighed the evidence of Christianity? *Second,* have I demanded that the evidence meet standards which are not at all suitable to type of evidence that a historical religion would be bound to have? *Third,* if it did conform to the standard would I immediately accept Christ, and endeavor to change my life wherein it is out of harmony with His will? Would I leave all to follow him, or would I "promptly raise the required standard of evidence or find some other point to argue about? This is the issue, and to focus attention on the absolute validity or otherwise of Christian evidence is to practice self-deception. The Christian does not stand for a religion which can answer every objection that the wit of man can raise, but for the teaching of Jesus Christ that all who are of the Truth find in Him their Saviour, Lord and God."[5]

Of those who think that the evidence is insufficient we may also ask: *If the Gospels are historical would that be enough evidence?* If they say no, then it is clear that it is not evidence that they lack but the willingness to receive evidence. The Gospels are historical, as has been shown in many works on Christian evidence and as the present author plans to establish in one of the volumes in this series. If the Gospels are not historical documents how can one establish any other documents as historical? They can be established in the same way that any documents of antiquity can be established; and the rejection of them is for reasons other than the idea that they are not historical. Some of those who maintain that the documents are not historical maintain it because their theory or theories demand such a verdict con-

---

[5]Dr. Robert E. D. Clark, *Conscious and Unconscious Sin,* pp. 166-168.

cerning the Gospels and not because historical research demands it. As Dr. John A. Scott wrote: "Sir Frederic G. Kenyon, Director of the British Museum, said that in excellence, in antiquity, and in closeness of time to the original issue, the manuscripts of the New Testament are in a class entirely by themselves."[6]

V. IN CONCLUSION

It is clear that the evidence for Christianity is of such a nature that it does bring to the surface what is in a man. If one is unwilling to follow Christ—because of the demand which such would make on his life—he can think up "reasons" to justify his failure to follow Christ. The real reason—his unwillingness—will be hidden from others by these reasons and finally even from himself because he does not think beyond these "reasons". Jesus, of course, has informed us that the Christian life involves effort. He has told men to count the cost, and of course one ought to count the cost of not following Christ. "Never once did He lure anyone to follow Him with promises of ease. Was it not that which kept men from following Him then, and is is not the same that keeps men from following Him now? In spite of all that is said to the contrary, the natural man has the lurking feeling that it would be too great a strain to follow Christ. Certainly our Lord once said and often implied that His yoke was easy and His burden light, but then He was calling men to take His yoke upon them, which meant that they were to follow him and risk everything which such following would entail. They would then find that the burdens they would have to bear, though heavy in themselves, would really be light and easy because He would be bearing the heavy end."[7]

Those who do not want to put forth the effort which is necessary to follow Christ will not be compelled by the evidences of Christianity. They will find it possible to rationalize and to attribute the fault to the evidences of Christianity instead of to themselves. And in doing so they not only reveal that they do not put the spiritual uppermost, but that they want to continue in the contrary attitude of life.

---

[6]*Luke, Greek Physician and Historian*, p. 32.
[7]Daniel Lamont, *The Anchorage of Life*, p. 177.

Chapter VII

THEORIES OF SCIENTISTS AND UNBELIEF

It is essential to remember that there is often a vast difference between the *facts* in the hands of a scientist and the *theories* by which he explains these facts. *All of the theories of a scientist are not scientific,* in that all of their theories are not proved and some of them are of such a nature that they cannot be proved; while some of them are absolutely contrary to evidence. There are also theories, held by some scientists, which are not essential in the interpretation and manipulation of materials. Just because they are held by scientists does not mean that they are scientific. The author does not in any way deprecate the contributions which have been made by scientists; and neither does he discourage scientific investigation. Scientists, however, are human and are subject to passions and prejudices like the rest of us mortals. Some of them, of course, have disciplined themselves better than have others.

Four of the unwarranted theories of some scientists will be discussed in this book. Two have been the stumbling block in the path of faith for multitudes of people. They have been the cause of and justification for unbelief in a measure that no other theories have been in our generation. These theories are first the dogma of uniformitarianism and second the creed called evolution. Not everything that can be said against these theories will be said in this chapter. Enough, however, will be said to show that they are unproved theories and that they have been the main-stay of unbelief in our generation. At a later date it is the author's intention to issue at least two volumes on these theories. One of them will be on *The Uniformitarian Dogma,* and the other will deal with some of the main arguments for the theory of organic evolution. However, as pointed out in this chapter, these two theories are closely related to one another, and the above dogma is one of the supports for the dogma of evolution. Third, size as the main standard of measurement is adopted by some scientists;

but only because, as we shall show, they do not think. Fourth, that the Bible is anti-scientific. Let us now turn our attention to the uniformitarian dogma.

A. THE UNIFORMITARIAN DOGMA

The tidal wave of unbelief, which is sweeping over the country today, by its very size leads some to have doubts concerning the Christian faith. And yet, the *number* of people who do not believe in the gospel is no argument against the truth of the gospel. That is, unless one wishes to hold to the obviously unsound position that truth is determined simply by the vote of the majority. It is also true that the number of unbelievers does not mean that there are a mulitude of good reasons why they should be unbelievers. The fact of the matter is that much of the unbelief today is due to the acceptance of a theory known variously as uniformity, uniformitarianism, or continuity. Once it is accepted in its extreme form, revelation and inspiration are rejected as a matter of course and without investigation. These are contrary to uniformitarianism and *therefore* they cannot be true, is the attitude of a multitude of unbelievers. Their anti-supernatural bias makes impossible, as long as tenaciously clung to, any fair consideration of the evidence for supernatural revelation.

I. A BRIEF HISTORY OF THE DOGMA

As geologists surveyed the remains of tremendous upheavals which had taken place in the earth they maintained that some causes or forces must have operated in times past, to produce these changes, which are not now operating. Around 1785 however, James Hutton, in his Theory of the Earth, advanced the theory that the causes which operated in times past to produce these changes are the same causes which now operate on the earth. The present, he argued, is the key to the past and if we want to know the causes which produced the tremendous changes in the earth we need only examine those causes which are now producing changes. Hutton's theory was given world-wide influence through the work of Charles Lyell. Today this theory is,

with some slight modifications, accepted as one of the funda
mental principles of geology.[1]

II. The Influence of the Theory

The theory has had an influence both on the doctorine of
evolution and on the world's attitude toward the *supernatural*.
T. H. Huxley, an agnostic evolutionist, maintained that Lyell
and his theory were the chief agents in smoothening the road
for Darwin. For evolution is simply an extension to the biological
world, the world of living things, of the principle of uniformity
which Hutton and Lyell applied to the physical world.[2] All living creatures, including man were produced by the laws which
we now see operating and not by a creation by God which is
different from anything now taking place.

This doctrine led to the denial of miracles. Miracles claim
to be something unique, something distinct from that which is
produced by the ordinary workings of the laws of nature which
now work around us. As Rogers, Hubble, and Byer put it—in
their textbook which is used in some state universities—"miracles
do not occur."[3] *They admit, however, on the same page that
uniformity is one of those assumptions which can not be proved
to have always operated.* And it is on the basis of just this assumption that so many people reject the Bible, and all the evidence for the supernatural intervention of the Divine into the
so-called natural course of things. It is the core—under the name
of continuity—of the philosophy of John Dewey which denies
the divine and supernatural and makes man one end of a long
line, of which matter is the other end. His adherence to this
doctrine, and his influence on educational thought in this country,

---

[1]L. M. Davies, *The Bible and Modern Science,* 3rd Edition, London:
Pickering and Inglis, pp. 150, 151, 152, 207-208. Professors J. Speed
Rogers; Theodore H. Hubble; and C. Francis Byer, *Man and the Biological
World,* New York: McGraw-Hill Book Company, Inc., 1942, pp. 294-296.

[2]Davies, *op. cit.,* pp. 151-152. Lyell, however, did not extend the
theory and try to make it account for the origin of man. See *Principles of
Geology.*

[3]*Op. cit.,* p. 306.

is brought out by the present writer in his dissertation on *A History of Pragmatism in American Educational Thought*.[4]

It is such an accepted theory in scientific thought that one English author stated that the evidence which seemed to point to a creation of the universe, suddenly at some time past, could not be accepted because it would violate the doctrine of continuity. "No explanation could be accepted as scientific which involved such a breach of continuity."[5] To the present author it has seemed that science ought to fit facts instead of crucifying facts in order to make them fit a theory, but such is the popularity of the theory that multitudes of scientists go wrong, in so far as accepting evidence for the supernatural is concerned, because of their blind adherence to this theory.

These uniformitarians would certainly be the best of law-abiding citizens if they adhered as strictly and rigidly to the laws of the land as they do to the law of uniformity which they have unwarrantedly extended to embrace creation and all of life. One wonders who passed this law. What legislative body formulated it and decreed that at no time in the past, and at no time in the future, could there be any violation of this law! Where did they get the power to enforce it and to make it retroactive as well as law for all ages and events to come! How did it become such a crime to maintain that there is any exception to this law? No, gentlemen, such strict adherence to uniformity is itself illegal for it ignores evidence.

III. The Christian's Position

The Christian affirms, of course, that there are laws operating in the universe. He realizes that there is uniformity. He does not put biscuits in the oven one day and expect them to become warm, and put them in the next day, under the same conditions, and expect them to freeze. He maintains, however, that uniformity does not extend to the extreme position that denies

---

[4]A copy of this dissertation may be found in the University of California library, Berkeley, and in Harding College library, Searcy, Arkansas.

[5]Quoted by E. W. Battersbey, *Transactions of the Victoria Institute*, Vol. LXXVI (1944), p. 22.

creation, and the miracles recorded in the Bible. The fact that God has expressed himself in natural laws does not mean that He could not otherwise express Himself and exercise His will in bringing to pass events which would not have come to pass through the ordinary expressions of his will in what we call laws of nature. God has intervened, as the evidence shows, in creation, in the History of Israel, in the Incarnation, in Redemption, and in the other things connected therewith.

IV. The Miraculous Is Not Impossible

Let the scientist allow Christians the same freedom that he claims for himself, the freedom to make basic assumptions. He admits that the doctrine of continuity is an assumption which cannot be demonstrated to be all-embracing. Let us assume that God is. We are convinced, of course, that in many ways this belief may be tested, and that the evidence for it is overwhelming when fairly considered. The overwhelming majority of mankind, including most evolutionists, accept this as a reasonable assumption and they believe that God is. Since God is, then certainly His mind and will can act on matter and on humanity. For since man can exercise his mind and will and bring to pass events, cause them, which would not come to pass if man did not exercise his will; then God certainly can do the same since He is immeasurably greater than man. *Where He intervened, and made it known to man, that intervention* would involve the miraculous and be revealed to man as such.

F. Bettex, well said: "Why not look upon a miracle as that which it professes to be, as that apart from which it would be no miracle—as something happening outside the limits of the known laws of nature, be it an occurrence in obedience to higher laws, be it an arbitrary and supernatural intervention of God. From this simple position with regard to a miracle . . . two things follow: First, the absurdity of denying it. To maintain that no miracle has ever taken place, that such a thing is impossible, is nothing else than to maintain we know all the forces and laws and possibilities in the universe! For four thousand years we have noted and investigated so thoroughly every single fact in the life of the individual and of the nation, every phenomenon of nature and the universe in general, that we are able to determine what is possible and what impossible. During this brief span of time we have been able to draw certain and infallible conclusions as to all that has happened and ever will happen . . ."

"The second result that follows from the above definition of a miracle is the impossibility of scientifically disputing it. A miracle is altogether outside the province of scientific criticism (which deals with that which can be repeated when the physical causes are right. No one maintains that miracles are repeatable or that they were produced simply by bringing together certain physical conditions, J. D. B.). This was acknowledged by the great scientist, Tyndall, who was by no means a believer in the Bible, yet admitted that if there is a God he is almighty, and can therefore work miracles; and that miracles, if there is such a thing, have nothing to do with science, but lie outside her province. Quite true, we say, and would recommend this utterance of a man of the first rank to those of tenth rank who delight in confronting miracles with science . . ."[6]

The only question, then, which one raises with reference to miracles, is not whether or not it is in harmony with the dogma of uniformity. The question is: Is there *evidence* that God has miraculously intervened into the affairs of mankind?

That He has done so in the Bible is shown by the evidence which proves that the Bible is from God.[7]

V. The Dogma May Be Turned Against the
Evolutionist Who Denies Supernatural Intervention

If the dogma of uniformity is strictly adhered to evolution itself would be strictly impossible. For unless it can be shown today that life is being originated from non-living matter, then

---

[6]*Science and Christianity,* New York: Hodder and Stoughton, 1901, pp. 141-143.

[7]We commend Olinthus Gregory, *Christian Evidence,* for proof of the point, which some have denied, that the strength of the testimony to the miracles of Christ is no more weakened by the passage of time than is the strength of the testimony to the existence of Nero.

one must conclude that life never came from non-life and that evolution could not have taken place. *First,* evolutionists admit that the spontaneous generation of life from non-life has never been proved and that all the proof is to the effect that this doctrine is not true. Since it is not true now, the uniformitarian must say that it has never been true. Therefore, evolution itself could not get started without a miracle, without an exception to uniformity; for something must have operated in the past to produce life which is not now operating to produce life. *Second,* in harmony with this evolutionists admit that life comes only from life. They also admit that life has not always existed on the earth.[8] It follows, therefore, that some Supernatural Power, which had life, placed life on this earth for man could hardly come here in a rocketship. And even if he had, that would not solve the origin of life, but simply place the problem on another planet, and one would have the same problem as to how life originated there. *Third,* there is no proof that invertebrates are evolving into vertebrates for example. Since the present is the key to the past, so says the uniformitarian, it is evident that such never took place.

It is clear that the evolutionist himself must violate the dogma of uniformity to even get a workable *theory* of evolution.

VI. The Fundamental Error of Uniformity

The fundamental error of the dogma of uniformity, particularly as applied to the theory of organic evolution "is simply this," as the Duke of Argyll pointed out years ago "that all the theories of development ascribe to known causes unknown effects."[9]

VII. The Theory Upset by the Operation of Human Intelligence

It is a fact that human life and intelligence did not always exist on this earth. Even atheistic scientists, and most scientists are not atheists, admit that conditions on earth were once such

---

[8]Rogers, et al., *op. cit.,* pp. 202-203.
[9]*Primeval Man,* p. 44; quoted by Davies, *op. cit.,* p. 220.

as to make human life impossible. And yet, human intelligence today operates as a cause. He who denies this is blind and labels himself as unintelligent and as a mere thing which is acted upon by external forces, but who himself causes nothing. He is blind for if there is any fact it is that human intelligence can so manipulate things that results are brought into being which would not otherwise have appeared. The laws of nature, without human intelligence, would not have produced a Model-T, much less a Lincoln. And every book which is written to prove that man is without any freedom, and that intelligence cannot cause things, is itself a refutation of the author's position. For the author purposed such a book, and produced it. It would have never been purposed or produced by the laws of nature operating in matter apart from human intelligence. And, as we have said, he also labels himself as unintelligent and a mere thing, for he denies that he is an intelligent cause of anything and that all things done through him are done just as if the term intelligence, and what it stands for, had never been. But every moment of our lives we see evidence of human intelligence operating as a cause.

Since human intelligence did not always exist, it must be admitted that there is now operating a cause which did not always operate in all times past. And what is said of intelligence, may also be said of life itself. Life producing life is a cause which has not always operated on this globe.

Since there is this much breach of the dogma of continuity it is difficult to see why one should blindly adhere to it and let it prejudice his mind against the evidence for the supernatural origin of the Bible.

VIII. The Bible Destroys the Dogma

The Bible can be shown to be the work of a superhuman mind, and since it clearly teaches that miracles have taken place it proves that the dogma of uniformity cannot be true. This is true not only with reference to the Bible in general, but with reference to Jesus Christ in particular. It breaks down when one tries to apply it to Christ. As C. A. Row has shown, "Jesus Christ (is) not the result of the action of those forces which energise in the production of man, but (is) a manifestation of a superhuman power."[10]

IX. The Bible Predicted the Uniformitarian Dogma and the Denial of the Miraculous Which Is Based on It

It doubtless comes as a surprise to the unbeliever that the New Testament predicted just such a dogma and just such a denial of miracles on the basis of the dogma. It should at least begin to shake their confidence in their extreme position. For how did the writer of one of the books of the New Testament know that such a condition would one day exist. Especially when even most unbelievers—for example, Bertrand Russell in his *History of Western Philosophy* where he discusses, in connection with Christianity, Gibbon's five "causes" for the spread of Christianity—admit that in the first century the people believed that there were supernatural interventions.

Centuries ago Peter wrote to Christians as follows: "This second epistle, beloved, I now write unto you; that ye may stir up your pure minds by way of remembrance; that ye may be mindful of the commandment of us the apostles by the Lord and Saviour: knowing this first, that there shall come in the last days scoffers, walking after their own lusts, and saying, Where is the promise of his coming?" We pause here to observe that the Christians would be teaching, of course, that Jesus Christ was coming again to bring salvation to the righteous and to recompense tribulation to the wicked (Heb. 9:27-28; 2 Thess. 1:6-11).

This teaching would be based on supernaturalism for if Christ is coming again it means that He is more than man. For who is expecting that in the natural course of things a man who died two thousand years ago is coming again? If He is coming again He is right with reference to what He taught for He taught that He would come again. And His coming again is based on the fact that His first coming was supernatural; that

---

[10]*A Manual of Christian Evidence*, London: Hodder and Stoughton, 1889, pp. 59-74.

death did not hold Him; that after His resurrection He ascended to heaven; and there He is to remain until the time for His second advent. All this, we say, is based on supernaturalism and constitutes a denial that things have always continued as they are now operating. It also constitutes a denial that things will always continue in the future as they are now. For since Christ's first advent was accompanied by supernatural manifestations something took place then that is not taking place now; and when He comes again forces will operate of which the present natural laws know nothing. But scoffers are denying His coming, and Peter said that in their mockery they would ask: Where is the promise of His coming?

On what do they base their mockery and their scoffing question? Peter states the basis for their mockery in the same verse. "Where is the promise of his coming? *for* since the fathers fell asleep *all things continue as they were from the beginning of the creation.*" (2 Pet. 3:1-4) Peter continues and teaches, among other things, that they have ignored the evidence for the flood; that the fact that Christ has not yet come is not a sign that He will not come, but is simply a manifestation of the grace of God which gives men additional time in which to repent; and that Christ will come again and that the earth will be destroyed by fire.

The thing, however, with which we are concerned is the reason on which they are basing their denial of His second advent. They deny it because they maintain that things are now as they have always been. "All things continue as they were from the beginning of the creation," this is their reason. "There is no mistake about this rendering. The Greek word arche, meaning 'beginning' is there used: so that Creation itself is clearly meant to be involved in the continuity of present-day process."[11] H. E. Dana, and Julius R. Mantey, state that the tense of "continue" indicates that perpetuity is implied by it. In commenting on the "static present tense" in Greek, they wrote: "the present tense may be used to represent a condition which is assumed as perpetually existing, or to be ever taken for granted as a fact." One

[11]Davies, *op. cit.,* p. 160, footnote.

of the references which they give to illustrate this is 2 Pet. 3:4, "While this use is rare, it is nevertheless fully significant of the genius of the tense. The idea of progress in a verb of being. This use is practically the present of duration applied to a verb of being."[12]

These scoffers maintain that there has been no supernatural intervention in times past because they assume that the only processes which have ever worked are those which now work. Such miracles are not being wrought now. Thus they were never wrought! There will be no supernatural manifestations in the future for the processes which now work will continue to work for all time to come. They thus extend their doctrine back to include creation itself and forward to include all future events. "*Their* doctrine of 'creation,' therefore, is one which dispenses with God's interventions, and appeals to present-day processes alone, as being perfectly sufficient of themselves to explain the origin and development of everything in nature. In other words, their doctrine is identical with the doctrine of evolutionists." "See, too, how these people are represented as making their statements with the greatest assurance——They do not say that all things continue as 'they are held to have continued,' from the beginning of creation, but that they continue 'as from' that beginning. They admit of no doubt upon the matter. Although they extend Uniformity back to the very beginning of creation, and thus flatly contradict Genesis, they speak as though they were quoting 'clear and demonstrative knowledge.' Thus an illegitimate extension of Uniformity is given out, by these men, as the purest science."[13] It reaches back through the time of Christ and even embraces creation itself, and thus denies all the supernatural manifestations set forth in the Bible. And, of course, if there was nothing supernatural about Christ's first coming, He was not what He claimed to be and thus He will not be coming again. So sure of this doctrine of continuity are these modern deniers of the supernatural that Edward Clodd wrote: "Evolution knows only one heresy—the denial of

---

[12]*A Manual Grammar of the Greek New Testament*, New York: The Macmillan Company, 1928, p. 186.

[13]Davies, *op. cit.*, pp. 160-162.

continuity."[14] "Nothing else matters to the evolutionists. Once you grant the fundamental dogma of continuity, all modern apostasy will follow inevitably from it, exactly as declared in Scripture eighteen centuries ago."[15]

It is well to call to the reader's attention the fact that the King James translation, which clearly states this doctrine of continuity, was made in 1611, long before James Hutton, Lyell, and others popularized the doctrine of continuity. "Although no hint of the modern dogma of Continuity had then appeared; our translators—with nothing but the inspired Text to guide them—produced the perfect anticipation of modernist unbelief, actually employing the very word 'continue,' which so peculiarly characterises it today."[16]

By this time it should be clear to the reader that the tidal wave of unbelief, which has swept some portions of the religious and scientfic world, goes back to this doctrine of continuity. It is this anti-supernatural bias, and not any lack of evidence for the Bible, which has led multitudes to renounce the Bible and to explain it away. It is its supernatural claims which immediately discredit it in their minds for their bias leads them to deny, even without examination, all evidence for revelation. Let us not be unsettled by this vain bit of philosophy of man, but remain steadfast on the rock of the evidence for the Lord Jesus Christ.

B. THE THEORY OF ORGANIC EVOLUTION

The theory of organic evolution has been seized on by unbelievers to justify their unbelief. Evolution, not God, they maintain, is the cause of the plants and of all living things. It is true that those who deny the existence of God must fall back on some form of the theory of evolution in order to explain things. It is not true, however, that evolution actually explains things for in the first place evolution cannot be proved—the facts do not support it; and in the second place even evolution does not necessarily deny God for it could be maintained that such was the mode of

---

[14]*Pioneers of Evolution,* p. 37; quoted by Davies, 163.

[15]Davies, *op. cit.,* p. 163.

[16]*Ibid.,* p. 163.

divine creation; and futhermore, evolution does not tell you the *cause* of evolution; i. e. that which produced the changes.[17]

Nevertheless, it is true that the desire to get away from the idea of God has made the theory of evolution very acceptable to many unbelievers. As Morton wrote: "To get away from the supernatural and display the needlessness of God has undoubtedly been one of the impulses which has driven mankind so largely along the evolutionary paths of thought. Prof. H. F. Osborn, one of the very protagonists of Evolution today (though he admits that 'the old paths of research have led nowhere'), says frankly, 'from the period of the earliest stages of Greek thought man has been eager to discover some natural cause of Evolution and to abandon the idea of supernatural intervention in the course of nature'[18]: and when he himself speaks of Law directing Evolution he only means some principle contained in organisms, an evolution by resident forces, and says: 'We may first *exclude the possibility* that it acts either through supernatural or teleological interposition through an external creative power' (p. 10). Like most of the ancient Greek evolutionists he believes in some sort of spontaneous generation of life. All thinkers have to reckon with this strange bent of the human mind to convince itself of the needlesness of God."[19]

A complete, detailed refutation of the theory of evolution is not contemplated in the following paragraphs. This is being reserved for other works; but enough will be said in order to show some of the difficulties which evolutionists have not and cannot overcome. They are not difficulties which merely embarrass the theory, but which demolish it.

I. THE THEORY HAS NOT BEEN DEMONSTRATED

At some place or other in almost any book on evolution the writer will admit that the theory of evolution has not been demonstrated; although in the rest of the book he may write as if it is

[17]See W. H. Turton, *The Truth of Christianity.*

[18]*Origin and Evolution of Life*, p. 9.

[19]Dr. Harold Christopherson Morton, *The Bankruptcy of Evolution,* London: Marshall Brothers Limited, pp. 37-38.

firmly established and that only the ignorant, or the prejudiced reject it. This author has in his notes a number of statements from evolutionists who admit that it is simply a faith with them and in some cases they admit that they believe that the theory *must* be true because to them the only alternative, special creation, is clearly incredible.

II. The Origin of Life

No one has been able to produce a living organism out of in-organic matter. All efforts to estabish the doctrine of spontaneous generation have failed; and evolutionists will admit that all life today comes from life. Thus evolution breaks down before it gets started.

III. The Fact of Mutations

While it is true that man has been able to produce different varieties of wheat; better breeds of milk cows; and variations in such insects such at the fruitfly; these facts do not prove the theory of evolution. In the *first* place these experiments start with liv-ing things. *Second,* these do not prove what has happened in the past; especially they fail to prove a theory which does not start with life, but with matter. *Third,* these mutations are not at all the transmutations which would be necessary in order to establish the dogma of evolution.

IV. The Unbridged Gaps

The theory calls for impossible transformations to bridge the numerous gaps between the lowest forms of living things and the highest forms. It is not just a question of *the* missing link, but of innumerable missing links. Neither the fossils in the rocks nor the living creatures on earth fill these gigantic gaps, such as the gap between invertebrates and the vertebrates.

V. The Fallacy of Hasty Generalization

The evolutionists are guilty of the fallacy of a hasty gen-eralization. They generalize and draw sweeping conclusions which are not at all justified by the facts. To generalize and conclude, because there is variation within species, that the theory of organic evolution—which embraces the development from non-life to life, and then gradually to the highest forms of life, by forces resident within matter—is an excellent illustration of a crude, hasty generalization. Nothing in the facts warrant such a sweeping conclusion.

VI. The Fallacy of Proving the Wrong Conclusion

Another logical fallacy in which the evolutionist is involved is that of proving the wrong conclusion. He is like the Irishman who wanted to prove, contrary to the testimony of three eye-witnesses that he was not guilty of stealing, because he could produce thirty witnesses that did not see him do it. Just so the evolutionist points to the mutations of, for example, the fruit fly. All that the evidence proves is that there are mutations which can be produced in the fruit fly. That is the only conclusion that such evidence supports. The evolutionist however, proves the wrong conclusion and maintains that such things prove that the theory of organic evolution is thereby demonstrated.[20]

C. THE INSIGNIFICANCE OF MAN

Unbelievers have sometimes pointed to the vast expanse of the sky, with its countless stars and its unlimited expanse; and then they point to man: how small, how insignificant he is; and how short his life. Man, they say, is so insignificant that God, if there is a God, would not be interested in him, as the Bible teaches that He is interested in man. As the poet said:

---

[20]There are other things which could be mentioned but these are sufficient to indicate that the theory of evolution is simply a theory, and not a demonstrated fact. The reader who wants thoroughly to investigate the theory, or to be more accurate the *theories* of evolution, should consult the books recommended in the section following the remarks on "Faulty Reading." In addition to these we recommend the pamphlet on *Evolution* which may be ordered for twenty cents from the International Christian Crusade, 366 Bay St., Toronto, 1, Canada. On pages 92-93 a list of recommended readings will be found. This pamphlet is excellent to circulate among college students who are having difficulties because of the theory.

"Stately purpose, valour in battle, splendid annals of army and fleet,
  Death for the right cause, death for the wrong cause, shouts of triumph,
    sighs of defeat,
  Raving politics, never at rest while this poor earth's pale history runs:
  What is it all but the murmur of gnats in the gleam of a million mil-
    lion suns?"

Of course, we might ask: If this is the true picture of man's value, then there is not much reason that man should take any consideration of man. What would it matter that the gnat's murmur ceased today instead of tomorrow?

But this is not the true picture; reason shows that the measuring standard is wrong. It is true that in some ways man is insignificant. This was recognized by the psalmist, but knowing God's standard of measurement as revealed in God's care for man, he did not stop with the view of the littleness of man in comparison with the stars of the heavens.

"When I consider thy heavens, the work of thy fingers, the moon and
    the stars, which thou hast ordained;
  What is man, that thou art mindful of him, and the son of man, that
    thou visitest him?
  For thou hast made him a little lower than the angels, and hast crowned
    him with glory and honor.
  Thou madest him to have dominion over the works of thy hands; thou
    hast put all things under his feet:
  All sheep and oxen, yea, and the beasts of the field;
  The fowl of the air, and the fish of the sea, and whatsoever passeth
    through the paths of the seas." (Psa. 8:3-8)

God's mindfulness of man overwhelms us, especially when we recognize that God commendeth His own love toward us in that while we were yet enemies Christ died for us. (Rom. 5:8-10).

But back to the logic of the person who contrasts the size of man with the size of the universe and concludes that man is of no value. If the individual will remember that he himself is not quite enough of a fool to make size the supreme measuring rod of life, why should he think that God would make it the standard of value? "A little courageous thinking will show us that this logic of mere size—the logic of the foot-rule and of the grocer's scales—has no relevancy in the realm in which man stands. It does not run in the great spiritual kingdoms to which he belongs.

"We act on this belief every day in the circle of our lives. We refuse to be bullied by mere scale. In the realm of love, for example—and that realm is the highest, the sweetest, and the noblest we know—mere physical bulk has no relevance. It might almost be described as an impertinence. Will any mother consent to have the value of her child measured in inches, or assessed in pounds avoirdupois? She may be told that the house is a thousand times bigger than the baby, and this is true. But in love's realm the argument of the foot-rule does not count. In the scales of a mother's values all the Himalayan and Alps of the planet are less than her infant!"[21]

What if the stars are numberless and the expanse is limitless, it is still man who charts the heavens, and thinks about the stars. Man is superior to them; he sees them, they do not see him. He is living, intelligent, and spiritual; but they are lifeless matter. "Man belongs in the last analysis to the moral order. This is his essential characteristic and distinction. He can not only think; he can love and will. His character is the field—or, it may be—of the greatest moral qualities, of love imperishable, of goodness, of righteousness. In the realm of the natural affections as we have seen, and in the kingdom of the intellect, material bulk has neither value or relevancy. How much more must this be true in the yet loftier world of moral character!"[22]

Thus it is that a little reflection indicates that the size of man, physically speaking, has nothing to do with the question of faith in God. It should not be used as a hindrance to the growth of faith.

Lest, however, the reader conclude that no one, of any note has been blind enough to measure man and his value by the mass of the stars, etc., we quote from the well known English unbeliever, Bertrand Russell. In *What I Believe* he wrote: "The philosophy of nature must not be unduly terrestrial; for it, the earth, is merely one of the smaller planets of one of the smaller stars of the Milky Way. It would be ridiculous to warp the philosophy of nature in order to bring out results that are pleasing

---

[21]W. H. Fitchett, *The Unrealized Logic of Religion* (London: Charles H. Kelly, 1905, pp. 58-59).

[22]Ibid., p. 61.

to the tiny parasites of this insignificant planet. Vitalism as a philosophy, and evolutionism, show, in this respect, a lack of sense of proportion and logic relevance. They regard the facts of life, which are personally interesting to us, as having a cosmic significance, not a significance confined to the earth's surface. Optimism and pessimism, as cosmic philosophies, show the same naive humanism; the great world, so far as we know it from the philosophy of nature, is neither good nor bad, and it is not concerned to make us either happy or unhappy. All such philosophies spring from self-importance, and are best corrected by a little astronomy."[23] That Russell failed to see, with his keenness of mind, the fallacies involved in this measuring rod for the value and importance of man, is another indication of the fact that men become extremely blind through their passions and prejudices. When we consider the Bible and astronomy we do not draw the hopeless conclusion that Russell has drawn; instead we stand amazed, with the psalmist David, that God has been mindful of man. Instead of being dwarfed by the heavens, we see them declaring the glory of God and "forever singing as they shine, the hand that made us is divine." Russell's unbelief is not due to the immensity of the universe, however, but to other things such as the carnal condition of his heart, as is indicated by his remarks concerning morality, in *What I Believe*. It is the author's intention to deal with these remarks in the book on the consequences of unbelief; for immorality is both a cause and a consequence of unbelief.

IV. IS THE BIBLE ANTI-SCIENTIFIC?

In a book on *Science and the Scriptures* it is the author's intention, the Lord willing, to deal in detail with the charge that the Bible is unscientific and that it has tended to discourage scientific research. Here, however, we shall say only enough to indicate that the Bible itself has encouraged the study of nature, although some theologians may have departed from the Bible from time to time and have failed to encourage it. This, of course, is not the fault of the Bible, but of those who misrepresent it.

[23]London: Kegan Paul, Trench, Trubner and Co., Ltd., 1925, pp. 23-24.

The book of Job alone contains several encouragements to study nature, and even sets before mankind some questions with which we still wrestle. To some who claimed great knowledge Job said: "No doubt but ye are the people, and wisdom shall die with you." (Job 12:1). Then he invited them to study nature. "But ask now the beasts, and they shall teach thee; and the birds of the heavens, and they shall tell thee; or speak to the earth and it shall teach thee; and the fishes of the sea shall declare it unto thee. Who knoweth not in all these, that the hand of Jehovah hath wrought this . . ." (Job 12:7-9). Those who accept the in-vitation to study the beasts will be led into the field of biology; those who consider the marvels manifested in bird life invade the field of ornithology; those who carefully listen to the earth are geologists; and those who listen to the fishes of the sea long enough become expert ichthyologists.

In another place (38:1-), God asked Job a number of ques-tions, and they still, in the main, stump scientists. Nowhere does God's word discourage investigation which is conducted in the right attitude and which is desirous of discerning truth and not of supporting error. The Christian can enter into every field of legitimate scientific work that any other individual can enter into, and all without one word of condemnation from the Bible. Faith in God does not discourage him in his search for truth in the natural world; instead he is encouraged by the thought that in doing so he is finding what God has placed before man and in-vited him to investigate.

In drawing this chapter to a close it is the author's conviction that these theories of some scientists, which have been used to destroy faith in the Bible, are theories which are held not be-cause of the evidence but in spite of the lack of evidence for them and in the face of evidence which is against them. Scientists, some of them, and their theories may oppose the Bible at times but in such cases the conflict is between the Bible and the preju-dices of scientists, and not between the facts and teachings of the Bible and the facts of science.

The following chapter on "The Bible and The Intellect" also refutes the charge just considered.

CHAPTER VIII

THE BIBLE AND THE INTELLECT

There are some people who reject Christianity because they claim that it is anti-intellectual; that it deprecates mind and appeals to the emotions; that it neglects the intellect and appeals to credulity. Their charges are not a reflection on Christianity but an indication of their abysmal ignorance of true Christianity. It may be true that there are cults which throw away their mind and give full-throttle to the emotions, but any real student of the Bible recognizes that this is not true Christianity. It may be true that some groups appeal to credulity but Christianity does not, as we have shown in the chapter on that subject.

I. CHRISTIANITY DOES NOT FETTER THOUGHT

Christianity calls on man to think, to examine evidence, in becoming a Christian. After he becomes a Christian he is under obligation to prove all things and hold fast to that which is good (1 Thess. 5:21). The range of things, on which Christians are invited and commanded to think, is vast enough to furnish a full curriculum of study for this life. As Paul wrote: "Finally, brethren, whatsoever things are true, whatsoever things are honorable, whatsoever things are just, whatsoever things are pure, whatsoever things are lovely, whatsoever things are of good report; if there be any praise, think on these things." (Phil. 4:8).

Christianity challenges men to think on the most serious and far reaching questions which can confront man, *and which do confront every man*. Questions such as: What is man? What is God like? What is the origin and destiny of man? What is the true way of life? Christ calls on men to think on the meaning of life, something which unbelief either ignores or makes a terrible mess of in its thinking. What greater challenge is there to the intellect than to think on the meaning of life? How insignificant all other questions are until this question is answered. As Dr. Clark pointed out, no one who has thought carefully can believe that it is right to drift thoughtlessly and aimlessly through life. And yet, some unbelievers are afraid to think seriously along this line, their thought is fettered with reference to the most important of all subjects. It may be because they are afraid that serious thought in the matter would lead them to the place where they would have to abandon cherished views or practices. It may be because they are afraid of the tidal wave of disillusionment and futility which would sweep over their lives if they really faced their own doctrine that life is utterly meaningless and purposeless.

Christianity does not fetter thought, but even if it did would it not be better for thought to be fettered with reference to geology, for example, than with reference to life's meaning and morality. Such alternatives are not before Christians for they may think deeply on all these things. The unbeliever, however, generally finds his thought fettered with reference to the most fundamental things.[1]

And yet these persons maintain that the Christians are the ones who are afraid to think, when they as a general rule are afraid to think long and seriously on the most vital of all questions, the question of the meaning and purpose of life. We utterly repudiate the suggestion that true Christianity fetters thought, that it is anti-intellectual; and we maintain that the teaching of Christianity itself, and its effects wherever it has been allowed to have its way, prove that Christianity does not fetter thought. That is, it does not fetter thinking about the truth and all wholesome thinking although it certainly fetters thought where it ought to be fettered, i. e. with reference to impure, lustful, hateful, wicked, thoughts. It fetters thought only where it needs to be, and it needs to be fettered in the very places where unbelief would unfetter it and give it free reigns to think on sinful things with the view of enjoying and participating in them. We do not mean, of course, that all unbelievers spend all of their time thinking on such things; not at all, for often their patterns of thought are shaped by other forces than unbelief. But we do maintain that in so far as the influence of unbelief on morality is concerned it encourages the

---

[1]*Conscious and Unconscious Sin,* pp. 164-166.

thinking of things that are unwholesome, as we shall show in the book, which we plan to write and publish later the Lord willing, on the consequences of unbelief.

II. The Extreme "Scholarly Detachment" Is Not Intellectually Commendable

It is a gross misconception of the position of the intellect to think that one must remain detached and non-committal. And yet some have this attitude and reject Christianity as anti-intellectual because conversion to Christianity implies that the intellect is no longer detached and characterized by a disinterested manipulation of its credentials and teaching. To be passionately devoted to something would seem to them to be a stain on the purity of aloof intellectualism. Such, of course, is not the case. It is anti-intellectual for the intellect to ignore the claims and the testimonies of man's moral consciousness; of man's emotional nature; of man's consciousness; of man's spiritual needs; and all the other facts which call for faith in Christ. And once the intellect has seen that these facts do call for faith it is a crime against the intellect to fail to be whole-heartedly devoted to Christ and the spiritual and physical welfare of humanity.

Dr. Charles Wordsworth has written penetratingly of extreme "scholarly detachment."

"Very nearly akin to this intellectual indolence," he wrote, "is the top dispassionate candor on which some skeptics plume themselves, as if it were the best method of attaining religious truth. They seem to forget that revelation comes to them, if it comes at all, from above, not from below, and from a Power in whose presence fear is a duty. If it exist at all, which is the question before them, it is a gift for which they ought to be thankful, not a suppliant upon their charity. They tell us that it is their first duty to preserve their minds from prejudice in favour of revelation; that they are responsible for the legal purity and judicial impartiality of their reason, which is to them the sole arbiter of truth. And so they exclude all hope of finding revelation, lest it should delude them into credulity, and all fear of losing it, lest they should be frightened into superstition. The fact is, that in so jealously guarding the supremacy of reason, they are really wronging what they profess to honour, they unduly limit the field of which it ought to take cognizance, and the position it ought to occupy. True, as all wise apologists of all ages remind us, 'Reason is a divine reality: and God who purposed, disposed and ordered nothing without Reason, wills that all things should be treated and considered with Reason.'[1] 'Reason is the only faculty we have wherewith to judge concerning anything, even Revelation itself.'[2] This is true, however, just because, and so far as, our reason is a guide of our life ever present with us, not a judge deciding in a court outside us. If it is to decide aright, it must take into account all the elements of our complex life, it must measure and balance all the forces that tend to preserve and extend our powers of will and feeling, as well as those which form our purely intellectual conclusions. Right reason cannot be guardian only of the interests of one faculty or of portion of the human soul, but is the director of the whole, and it must take cognizance likewise of the whole evidence offered by human na- ture. Thus the warm personal love felt by the soul of its Savior is evidence offered not by the intelligence, but by the heart. The impression of a divine voice speaking in a way which commands obedience in the pages of Holy Scripture, is evidence again offered, not so much by the intelligence as by the will and the conscience. But reason cannot, dare not, reject a consideration of either. Right reason on the contrary says, If there is a revelation it will touch the heart, it will speak to a conscience in just such a way as the Gospel does; and so far, I have the evidence I am bound to expect. Unless revelation did produce these effects, it would be irrational to accept it.

"If reason, however, restricts itself to merely intellectual evi- dence, the case of a man like the late John Stuart Mill accord-

---

[1]Tertullian, de poenitentia, par. 1.

[2]Butler, Analogy, part ii. chap. 3. Cp. Isaac Barrow, Sermon 2, Of Faith (Vol. ii, pp. 21-23, ed. 1683), and Sermon 13, Of the Christian Religion (p. 189), and my father's Letters to M. Gondon, ed. 2, pp. 49 following. Origin has sometimes been misrepresented as if he admitted Celsus' taunt that Christians believe on mere faith, without examination He really treats it as a *calumny* (c. Celsum, i. 9,13; iii. 50)."

ing to his own witness, shows the collapse.[3] Other faculties will have their rights somehow or other, or the man will perish. And even in the interests of pure intelligence, who can say that hope and fear, love and joy, are foes to be excluded? Did not hope enable Columbus to find America? Do not affection and inclination, as well as the expectation of success, play a real part in all scientific discovery? Do not feeling and taste give insight into character and argument? Does not experience show us daily that only he who loves can understand the language of love? Am I then to drive away all my best thoughts, all the quickening impulses of spiritual life, all my fears of losing man's highest good, and even turn against them and hate them as misleading falsities, because they do not happen to be arguments of a peculiar type, reducible to a certain form of syllogism? Am I to call this a reasonable state of mind? No, rather I should be utterly unreasonable if I did so. Surely it is much wiser to hold with the most profound of living poets.

'I say, the acknowledgment of God in Christ
Accepted by thy reason, solves for thee
All questions in the earth and out of it,
And has so far advanced thee to be wise.
Wouldst thou improve this to re-prove the proved?
In life's mere minute with power to use that proof.
Leave knowledge and revert to how it sprung?
Thou hast it; use it, and forwith, or die.
For this I say is death, and the sole death,
When a man's loss comes to him from his gain,
Darkness from light, from knowledge ignorance,
And lack of love from love made manifest.'

(R. Browning, A Death in the Desert)

---

[3]See his Autobiography, chap. v., "A crisis in my mental history." He quotes two lines of Coleridge (p. 140) as a true description of what he felt in his intense dejection:—

'Work without hope draws nectar in a sieve,
And hope without an object cannot live.'

Unfortunately, the religion to which he turned as an object was not the highest—a mere human affection, however tender. See p. 251, written shortly after the death of his wife:—"Her memory is to me a religion, and her approbation the standard by which, summing up as it does all worthiness, I endeavor to regulate my life."

This intellectual coldness seems, in fact, to be as sinful as intellectual indolence. Yet some people tacitly make the assumption that the intellect is outside morality; that you have but to follow your own bias and instinct in its sphere, and to disregard the consequences. This is, indeed, a very narrow system of ethics. Let us suppose a man to receive a letter purporting to come from his father, and containing a promise of something which he much desired, which would be a great comfort to him to have, and which the father was specially able to bestow. What should we say of such a man, if he submitted this letter to a purely intellectual test, and decided that the very suitability of the promise to his wants and wishes was a reason for doubting, if not for rejecting it? We should call him unfilial and brutal as well as stupid. And yet this is what these coldly-intellectual persons say with regard to what we tell them of their heavenly Father's message. In them 'lack of love' from love made manifest.' "

There are, of course, some unbelievers who are constantly looking for some word over which they can stumble, and thus excuse and justify themselves for not getting the point which is made in the argument, who will take the little word "faculties" and say, Ah, ha! See what a dumb individual that is basing his arguments on an outworn "faculty psychology." But the point still stands in Wordsworth's argument even if one takes out the term faculty, and calls these things general powers; specific powers; aspects of the unitary core of *human* life, for these are the things to which Wordsworth calls attention. Of course, if they want to deny heart, determination, and conscience, they can do as they want to do, but they will not thus change what is indicated by those terms; they will only intellectually deny certain truths on which even they act in everyday life.

Dr. Lamont has had some penetrating things to say concerning the extreme so-called scholarly detached attitude when considering the truth concerning God and the cross of Christ. Lamont did not deny, of course, that the evidence for God and Christ cannot be examined in a scholarly way. What he la-

---

³John Wordsworth, *The One Religion,* pp. 18-23.

mented was that men think that the scientific method is the only way to all truth, and that they thus cheat themselves out of certain vital truths.

"This narrow and intolerant view of the way in which the truth must be sought is the crowning vice of modern thought. When Science attempts to investigate God or even the human spirit by its own dispassionate method, its attempt is set at naught by both God and man. To treat a human being disinterestedly is to insult him. To treat God that way is the height of presumption. Mankind is to a large extent under the pitiful delusion that its only concern with God is to investigate Him. That is to make an idol of Science, and, unless this idolatry ceases, the idol will break mankind. The breaking process is already going on. God grant that the process may be stayed by the breaking of the idol! Science is like fire, an excellent servant but a devastating master.

"The modern intellectual situation is so serious that it would need a large volume to deal adequately with it. It must suffice here to point out that the disinterested attitude of Science is in its proper place in relation to objects. A full discussion of this point would reveal the fact that Science, because of its essential method, cannot probe the secret even of an object. If we knew a single object through and through, we should know the entire universe through and through. But let that pass. Let it be granted that Science is doing a legitimate and magnificent work in investigating objects as far as it can go. More power to it. But when God is regarded as merely object for investigation He is thereby dethroned in the heart of the man who so regards Him. It soon follows that man is dethroned from his rightful place in the universe. Then some inhuman monster gets to the top; millions are lured to follow him by his gilded boasts and promises; and leaders and followers alike are increasingly demoralized and dehumanized. All of them cease to be persons in the noble sense of that term. The disestablishment of God is bound to be followed by the disestablishment of man.

"In point of fact, even when a so-called inferior speaks to me, I dare not adopt the disinterested attitude *simpliciter*. I have to listen to a word addressed to me by a person. An object does not address me, but a person does. The scientific attitude is out of bounds when it is applied without qualification to anyone who addresses me. It is entirely out of bounds when it is applied to the Most High.

"The disinterested attitude to God implies that man is the judge of God and His Word. Thus man puts himself above God. He becomes his own idol and the inevitable consequence is that he dehumanises himself. To make a god of oneself is to become much less than a man. The greatest of the anicent pagans knew this well. They knew it from what they had seen of life. Presumption was with them the sin of sins and was always the precursor of a mighty fall. When Science is turned into an idol, it means that man is his own idol. He speaks about 'conquering nature' when the best that he can do is to understand nature a little better and put it into service of mankind. He boasts that Science is the saviour of mankind, while he knows that it can also be the destroyer. It is such presumption, with its attendant demoralisations, that may turn Science, which ought to be a blessing, into a curse.

"The refusal to acknowledge the living God and to listen to His Word is not peculiar to modern times. It is the bent of the natural man in all ages. Pride, self-will, self-complacency and reluctance to have the current of one's life changed are perennial marks of unregenerate man. The difference made by modern mentality is that now the natural man, if he feels the need of theortical support for his way of living, thinks that such is forthcoming in the modern way of thinking. He may not troube himself to test the strength of his intellectual buttress, but wishful thinking stands him in good stead. He finds it plausible when he hears that 'man is the measure of all things' and that 'our brains are there in order that we may think for ourselves.' All of which he interprets to mean that what cannot be seen by the light of his own little candle does not exist. He will believe nothing that he cannot prove. And so on. His ideas are partially true, but a half-truth is usually the chief enemy of the truth. This man evades the greatest issue of all, which may be expressed thus. Is there nothing which shines in its own light?"[4]

III. CHRISTIANITY IS A BLOW TO INTELLECTUAL PRIDE

The attitude that Christianity is anti-intellectual is often simply a reaction of pride to the blow which is dealt to it by Christianity. Man feels, at times, very sufficient of himself to direct properly his own steps. To acknowledge not only that he is morally weak but also that his intellect needs God's word in order for man to make the proper choices in life, and to attain to the true goal of life, is mortifying to this idea of self-sufficiency. And so to retaliate against this "insult" pride wants to label Christianity "anti-intellectual."

Christianity, however, is not anti-intellectual but gives to the intellect the answer to the most vital questions which arise in the mind of man. It is a spur, not a hindrance, to real thought. Indeed, "it is not inquiry, but a non-inquiring acquiescence in doubt, which is the peril of this day. It costs much to disbelieve; it requires submission to our God and His grace, to believe. The temptation of this age is to try to find a middle path between faith and unbelief; to say that 'there is much to be said on both sides'; to think that all things must be uncertain in themselves, because many of the persons around us are at sea as to all things, as if one thought all things to be in a whirl, because they seemed so to our neighbors who had dizzied themselves; to be browbeaten out of belief; to shrink from avowing a steadfast adherence to that which must be old because it is eternal, and which must be unchangeable because it is truth; to pick something out of revelation, which, it thinks, will not be gainsaid, and to relegate all else to be matter of opinion; an indolent, conceited, soft, weak, pains-hating, trifling with the truth of God."

"The battle must be fought. It is half-won, when any one has firmly fixed in his mind the first principle, that God is All-Wise and All-Good, and that man's own wisdom, although from God, is no measure for the Wisdom of God, and cannot sound its depth.

[4]Dr. Daniel Lamont, *The Anchorage of Life*, London: Inter-Varsity Fellowship 1940, pp. 153-157.

The criticism of rationalism is but a flimsy transparent veil, which hides from no eyes except its own, (if indeed it *does* hide it altogether from its own,) the real ground of its rebellion, its repugnance to receive a revelation to which it must submit, in order that it may see."[5]

Let us not permit intellectual arrogance to blind us to the fact that Christianity not only enlightens the intellect but also properly directs it, and thus determines fruits of thought, so that the mind of man does not become the source of diabolical plans for the destruction of humanity. What a reaping it would be for the intellect through pride to reject the only thing which can keep the intellect itelf from being destroyed.

Let us now turn to the objection that Christianity is impractical and antisocial in its nature and that thus it must be discarded for the welfare of humanity.

---

[5]E. B. Pusey, *Daniel the Prophet* (New York: Funk and Wagnalls, 1885), pp. 452, 453.

CHAPTER IX

IS CHRISTIANITY IMPRACTICAL AND ANTI-SOCIAL?

In a world in which there is much emphasis on the practical and on the improvement of social conditions, there are unbelievers who think that Christianity is impractical and anti-social and that therefore it is both out-of-date and false. The individualism of the gospel makes it anti-social in a generation which needs social cooperation, they reason.

I. IS CHRISTIANITY IMPRACTICAL?

Of those who reject Christianity because they say that it is impractical and will not work in the twentieth century, we ask: Just what is practical? And, to be specific, just what is it about the Christian faith that is impractical? Also what has been so practical about the way of life which has been lived by multitudes, apart from Christianity, up to now? The mess that the world is in; the danger in which man constantly stands in the presence of selfishness and greed; are all these things practical? Is hate of man for man; is lust; is dissipation; is jealousy; is envy; is blind wrath; is greed; is sin—which covers all the above and more too, practical?

It is true that to the man who wants to live for himself, or even for others while leaving God out of his life, Christianity cannot be very practical. As long as a man is unwilling to leave the lower for the highest; sin for holiness; the non-christian life for the Christian life; it is impractical. Multitudes, however, testify that it has been the practical way to peace of heart; hope, strength of character; and purpose in life. There are many others, who do not profess to be Christians, who maintain that unless we are willing to put into practice at least some of the principles for which Christianity stands, that more trouble and sorrow awaits the world; sorrow and trouble which the practice of Christianity would enable man to avert.

It is true of course, that men who choose to live the Christian life in a non-Christian world will have to pay whatever cost is involved. But anything is not discredited just because it costs something. And even as Christians pay that cost they are being spent in the service of humanity endeavoring to save and elevate them; they are reaping strength of character; and they are sustained by the hope of the life to come. The real question, however, is not does it cost something to be a Christian, but is Christianity true? Is it sustained by evidence? If it is, then the sincere and morally sensitive individual recognizes that he has an obligation to accept and abide by it regardless of whether or not he can see how it will work out in every possible situation in life. And even the unbeliever must concede that if there is any such thing as duty that one ought to do his duty when he see it regardless of whether or not it seems to be the practical thing at the moment. If Christianity is true it places man under obligation and presents both duties and privileges which cannot be turned aside from by a person with a snap judgement that Christianity is impractical. The facts are that no other way of life is really practical for both the life which now is and the assurance of the life which is to come.

The fact that the Bible emphasizes the practical aspects of things is seen in the use which is made of one of the distinctive Christian doctrines, i. e., that Jesus had once existed in the form of God, but that He was made in the likeness of man and died for us. The Bible sets this doctrine before us not for the purpose of satisfying our curiosity or giving Christians a subject for speculation. It is set before Christians for the very practical purpose of giving them an example of humility and service which encourges the like characteristics in them. After exhorting the brethren to unity and humility Paul said: "Have this mind in you, which was also in Christ Jesus: who existing in the form of God, counted not the being on an equality with God a thing to be grasped, but emptied himself, taking the form of a servant, being made in the likeness of men; and being found in fashion as a man, he humbled himsef, becoming obedient even unto death, yea, the death of the cross." (Phil. 2:5-7) To some people this may seem to be a lot of theoretical ideas, but not so to Paul or other Christians even unto this day.

Those who have studied the Bible recognize that the emphasis in the word of God is on that which is really practical for man. This fact has been admirably shown by Dr. Richard Whately in *Essays on Some of the Pecularities of the Christian Faith.* In his essay on the "Practical Nature of Revelation," Whately has shown that not only is the Bible such a book, but that it is in this respect in striking contrast with the false revelations given in other religions. It is also contrary in this emphasis, to a tendency in unregenerate human nature, and a tendency which is often evident even in the life of some believers, to theorize rather than walk in and practice the truth. In fact, in many cases, the perversions of Christianity have been in this direction, i.e., away from the practical to the speculative.[1]

II. IS THE GOSPEL TOO INDIVIDUALISTIC?

There are unbelievers who justify their unbelief by maintaining that the gospel of Christ is too individualistic, that it is interested in individual salvation, whereas the world today is in dire need of social salvation. Thus it is out of date. Although we commend efforts to improve the social welfare of man, we deny that it can be done except as individuals are improved. That is to say, as individuals are improved they will want to improve the lot of their fellowman; and so on until society as a whole feels the impact of the reformation which started in an individual soul. Lamont is right when he writes that "there has been much misconception about Christian 'individualism.' No doubt there have been people, claiming the name of Christians, who have lived self-contained lives; but a self-contained Christian is a contradiction in terms. If a man is not working for the highest good of his fellowman, it is safe to say of him that he is not in process of salvation. A follower of Christ has a heart which is filled with

---

[1]See also Dr. Robert E. D. Clark, *Conscious and Unconscious Sin,* p. 169. Also James D. Bales, *Soils and Seeds of Sectarianism,* pp. 89-108.

love to all men, and he cannot help doing his best for those whom he can influence. He witnesses for his Lord wherever he goes. It ought to be said boldly that a man like this is doing more to bring in a better social order than any reformer who cries aloud for some new system but who shows no kindness to his own poor neighbour. Robert Blatchford said long ago that when he was writing on the slums he liked to have a little slum child upon his knee. Academic theories of social improvement may be all very well, but commend me to the people who are shedding light and love around their own doorsteps. The Good Samaritan is a more effective social reformer than the priest or the Levite or even the soap-box orator."[2]

"It is to the New Testament and its heirs that we should turn if we would know the meaning of the 'individualism' of the Gospel. In point of fact nothing among us but the Gospel is universal, except it be sin and death for which the Gospel is the only remedy. It is instructive to note how there came to the ethical prophets of Israel the twofold Revelation that the One Righteous God was the God of all, and that because He was God of the whole earth He cared for each soul singly and alone. The Gospel is the completion of that Revelation. The rightful Lord of every man. The individual and universal aspects of His Lordship dare not be separated for God has joined them. It is grotesque to speak of a social gospel as if this were something apart from the Gospel of Love which is the only Gospel there is. The Gospel of Jesus Christ must find its lodgment in the individual heart if it is to appear on earth at all, and any social gospel which takes no account of the love-filled heart is a sham and no gospel. If the adjective is meant to emphasize the fact that the Gospel of Christ cannot be other than social, seeing it is the Gospel of Love, that is a different matter. But even so the adjective is apt to mislead."[3] In dealing with the social condition of others one must not forget the primacy of the spiritual, nor leave the impression on the financially poor that their only problem is a material one.

---

[2]*The Anchorage of Life*, pp. 190-191.
[3]*Ibid.*, p. 192-193.

No one who knows much about the New Testament can make the objection, and reject the New Testament on the basis of it, that it is so individualistic that it is not interested in the welfare of others. Was not the first commandment that men should love God with all their being, and the second one, like unto it, that they should love their neighbor as themselves? Did not John say that it was impossible to love God whom we have not seen and to hate our brother whom we have seen? "Hereby know we love, because he laid down his life for us; and we ought to lay down our lives for the brethren. But whoso hath the world's goods, and beholdeth his brother in need, and shutteth up his compassion from him, how doth the love of God abide in him? My little children, let us not love in word, neither with the tongue; but in deed and truth." (1 John 3:16-18) Did not Jesus say that the question of our conduct towards our fellows will be considered in judgment day? "Depart from me, ye cursed, into the eternal fire which is prepared for the devil and his angels; for I was hungry, and ye did not give me to eat; I was thirsty, and ye gave me no drink; I was a stranger, and ye took me not in; naked, and ye clothed me not; sick, and in prison, and ye visited me not. Then shall they also answer, saying, Lord, when saw we thee hungry, or athirst, or a stranger, or naked, or sick or in prison, and did not minister unto thee? Then shall I answer them, saying, Verily I say unto you, Inasmuch as ye did it not unto one of these least, ye did it not unto me. And these shall go away into eternal punishment: but the righteous into eternal life." (Matt. 25:41-46)

The New Testament holds up Christ the way, the truth, and the life. If men refuse to come to Him, what program can Christianity give to men who are content to remain on the lower level, to remain in sin. Even then, however, Christians help those very people who refuse to accept the highest standard. As leaven their teaching and good deeds work for the betterment of society. But Christianity has no program to recommend for man and for a good world *apart from God and submission to the will of God.* Christianity has no program for sinful men, who want to remain in sin, to make the world a paradise.[4] It can have no such program for sin is the reason that this world is not a paradise. How, then, if Christianity is from God, could it deal with the social problems of men, and work for the betterment of humanity, if it did not deal with the problem of sin which is the cause of which our social disorders are the symptoms. This sin is not only a sin of commission but also sin of omission. Not merely the sin of people doing that which is wrong, but the sin of failing to do that which is right. Men want a program which will make them comfortable in sin, but God has no such program for them. If there was such a program that program would be the worst thing that could be proposed, for men who were comfortable in sin would remain in sin and be damned by sin. It is only when they recognize that sin cannot bring true peace and joy that they are willing to accept Him who can forgive sin and cleanse them and place them on a higher level.

These individuals who condemn the gospel for being, as they call it, individualistic, and for not having the kind of social program which they want, really do not want to investigate and be influenced by the social implications of the gospel. No, they had rather hide behind their terms of contempt and justify their own unbelief by a process of rationalization. The main reason they do not like the social program of the gospel is that that program *starts with them.* They want sin's wages to be removed from the world, but sin and its pleasures they want. And when the gospel starts with them, *it starts with them at their sore spot,* i. e. their sinful selfishness. This sinful selfish in some cases may not always be manifested toward man, although in a measure it usually is, but it may be manifested toward God in that the individual is too self-willed to want to submit his life to the direction of God. He does not want to acknowledge his own incapacity and turn the direction of his life over to God. He thinks too much of himself to submit to such a surrender, and to stand the blow to his pride which the gospel brings by pointing out *that he is a sinner*

---

[4]This is not to deny, of course, that the gospel works for the good or even for those who reject it. It does work as leaven and elevate the standards of even unbelievers, as we have shown in the chapter dealing with the conduct of Christians.

and that one of the things that is wrong with the world is him and the sin which is in him. The gospel wants to start with the basic, primary, fundamental things—sin and sin in the life of each individual person—but sinful man wants to start with everything else; he wants to change systems without changing himself. And so, whether the unbeliever is always conscious of it or not, one of the ways in which sinful man hides from himself the truth about himself, (and hides his real reason for his antagonism to the gospel) is by trying to prove that the fault is with the gospel and that he himself is in the right. He is right because he sees the need for social reform; the gospel is wrong for it demands that first of all the reformer be reformed!

It is gratifying to hear corroboration of the fact that our primary problem is spiritual. It is from an unexpected source, a military one. General Douglas MacArthur said: "Military alliance, balances of power, League of Nations all in turn failed . . . We have had our last chance. If we do not now devise some greater, and more equitable system, Armageddon will be at our door. The problem basically is theological and involves a spiritual recrudescence and improvement of human character that will synchronize with our almost matchless advance in science, art, literature, and all material and cultural developments of the past two thousand years. It must be of the spirit if we are to save the flesh."[5] The problem is basically theological because our attitude toward our fellowman is determined, in the long run, by our conception of God. Strange as it may seem, man must reach to man through God if he is to reach man and to be at real lasting peace with man. To save the flesh we must go through the spirit. These words are filled with meaning. May men be stimulated by them to think.

Man, of course, must desire God himself and not merely His gifts. In other words, we cannot say that we need God to make this thing work and therefore we shall put God into it that God may work for us. Instead our recognition of the inability on our part, and the recognition of our utter dependence upon God, should lead us to seek Him. We seek Him because we realize

[5]Quoted in *Time*, p. 74, Sept. 10, 1945.

that we cannot live without Him. We acknowledge our need. We seek refuge in Him. We see not to use Him but to be used by Him. We seek not to make Him work for us but to give our lives to Him to work for Him; for the results of man's unaided efforts emphasize that He alone can make things work right. We surrender ourselves to Him for we recognize that we have lost the way and that we cannot find it in ourselves and by ourselves.

Even apart from the above facts, the following consideration alone disproves the accusation that Christianity is too individual-istic. The Christian sees other men not merely as fellowmen with whom he should deal according to the Golden Rule, but as *men for whom Jesus Christ died.* He sees them not as objects of hate; or lust; or selfish advancement; but as objects of redemption; men who are lost; who need Christ; and for whom Christ died. Lov-ing them, he is filled with unbounded good will toward them, be-cause Jesus Christ commended His love for them and for us in that He died for all. No one who understands this can ever ac-cuse the gospel of being too individualistic. The real trouble is that men have allowed *selfish* individualism and narrow, blind nationalism to come between them and the implications of the gospel of Christ; implications which show that the eternal good of all men is to be sought after by Christians.

The Golden Rule also proves that the Christian must be in-terested in the welfare of other people. It is not a negative rule which keeps one from hurting another, but at the same time re-maining unconcerned as to what happens to his fellowman; but is a rule which calls on Christians to be aggressive in goodness and take the initiative in helping others be what we are trying to be. "All things therefore whatsoever ye would that men should do unto you, even so do ye also unto them: for this is the law and the prophets." (Matt. 7:12). Of this John Dewey said over half-century ago: "The Golden Rule because it is positive, 'not attempt-ing to define any specific act, covers in its range all relations of man to man. It is indeed only a concrete and forcible statement of the ethical principle itself, the idea of a common good, or a community of persons.' "[6]

---

[6]John Dewey, *Outline of Ethics*, p. 205.

Those individuals who are too proud to admit humbly their sinfulness and their ignorance, and lack of lasting power, may perhaps be led to turn from their condemnation of the gospel as too individualistic if they will consider not only what has been said, but also the evidence of the leaven of faith in Christ where He has been preached. Such studies as the following show the social impact of faith in Christ, faith which in some instances was beclouded by some of the traditions of men, but which still produced many socially and morally desirable results. James S. Dennis' monumental three volume work on *Christian Missions and Social Progress* (New York: Fleming H. Revell Co., 1897); Charles Loring Brace, *Gesta Christi: or A History of Humane Progress Under Christianity* (New York: A. C. Armstrong and Son, 1883): and D. Coates, et al., *Christianity The Means of Civilization* "shown in the evidence given before a committee of the House of Commons on Aborigines (London: R. B. Seeley and W. Burnside, 1837). There are many other books on the subject, but Dennis' alone will contain enough evidence to convince the most doubtful that faith in Christ has exercised a tremendous leavening influence for good in the world.

CHAPTER X

THE PROBLEM OF EVIL

The unbeliever justifies his unbelief, at times, by pointing to the fact of evil in this world. He maintains that if God existed and was good that there would be no evil in the world; and that the fact of evil proves either that God does not exist or that God is either evil or morally indifferent. The unbeliever maintains that it is an evidence that God does not exist. In maintaining this, he is just as unreasonable in some ways as is the Christian Scientist who "solves" this question by maintaining that since God is good that there is no evil; no sin; no sickness; no death. Both are wrong, since God is and since mankind is faced with the fact of evil; the denial of the Christian Scientists only confirms the fact of evil for if there were no evil there would be no need for such a denial of it and the contention, as they do contend, that evil is an illusion. For even if that is all that it is, it is still a fact that the illusion itself would be an evil, for even as an illusion it has been real enough to man and has brought him sorrow and hurt.

If, as the unbeliever argues, the presence of evil is an argument against the existence of God, is it not strange that the Bible does not try to get rid of the fact of evil through some process of denial or at least to minimize it or give some long detailed explanation of the fact of evil. The Bible, however, not only does not minimize or deny evil but it emphasizes it; makes it stand out prominent; makes man increasingly conscious of it. It makes man more sin-conscious as is evidenced by the fact that where the influence of the Bible has gone men have become increasingly sensitive to sin, and have become aware of the evil that is in certain courses of conduct; things which they may have hithertofore regarded with indifference or even thought were good. The nearer men get to God, as is shown by the lives of the noblest saints, the more sensitive they are to the presence of sin in thir own lives and in the lives of others.

The awareness of the Bible to the fact of evil is, as Lamont points out, not the blow to Theism that some imagine it to be. "It is no reproach to Theism, but rather confirmation of its truth, that evil is the thorn in its flesh. For evil is the thorn in the flesh of humanity, and any system which does not reflect that fact of experience is bound to be inadequate. Pantheism, for instance, has no difficulty about the fact of evil for the reason that it has no moral seriousness. It fails to do justice to the sombre elements in the world and therefore its theory is inadequate to the total human situation. Christian Theism alone treats sin with passionate seriousness, as that which ought not to be. Sin is the enemy of God and man. This does not remove the difficulty but it at least shows how Theism, unlike all other systems, understands where the heart of the human difficulty resides."[1]

I. THE PRACTICAL NATURE OF REVELATION

The fact that the Bible recognizes evil, and that it does not present an elaborated theory as to the ultimate origin of evil, but instead shows man how to overcome evil, is in entire harmony with the characteristic of the Bible which may be labeled as "practical." That is, the revelations contained in the Bible are not of such a nature as to satisfy the speculative curiosity of mankind. It was not given for that purpose; it was revealed that man might know how to overcome sin and to live right. As God said to the children of Israel, the secret things belonged to Him, but the revealed things to the people that they might learn to do all the words of the law (Deut. 29:29). And that practical note is evident throughout the Bible, as Richard Whately has shown clearly in his *Essays on Some of the Peculiarities of the Christian Faith.* And thus with reference to the fact of evil, the Bible tells us what God is doing to help man overcome evil in his own life. And that, after all, is the practical thing. What matters it that the Bible does not give an elaborate theory of its origin; or go into a detailed theodicy; when it shows us how to deal with evil. That is what mankind needs to know; and to know that man does not

---

[1]Lamont, *op. cit.,* pp. 166-167.

need to have a great deal of information on the origin of evil or why God has allowed it to exist.

The Bible, however, does give us enough information for all practical purposes concerning both the entrance of moral and of physical evil into this world. In Genesis three the entrance of sin, moral evil, is dealt with. In the same chapter we are told that the curse, which followed the entrance of sin, affected nature also. Thus in dealing with man and nature today we are not dealing with them as they came perfect from the hand of God but as they have been marred by sin and the curse.[2]

II. The Problem of Good

It will be well for the unbeliever to ask himself how, in the type of universe which his theory constructs, man became conscious of the fact that evil is evil, and how that there could be good in the world. On their theory of moral, as we plan to show in the book on the consequences of unbelief, there may be such things as convenient and inconvenient, unpleasant and pleasant, that really there could be no such thing as evil or good. In this place, however, it is enough to remark, in the words of Lamont, that the unbeliever owes his present moral criteria, by which he condemns evil as evil and uses it as an argument against God's existence, to theism. "Mankind in general regards evil as an enemy. It holds evil to be the opposite of good. It must therefore be in possession of some standard of criticism by which it judges evil to be the denial of good. When a man with moral sensibility, but without faith, founds his objection to Theism on the fact that God permits cruelties to go on unchecked, (he assumes God in no way checks it, the Bible and experience teach that He does exercise certain checks, J. D. B.), he thereby employs a moral criterion. How did he come to possess that criterion? He may say,

---

[2]Dr. L. Merson Davies has dealt with the fact of the curse on nature in The Bible and Modern Science (Pickering and Inglis, Glasgow, Scotland) See Chapters VI-IX. Also his stimulating lecture delivered before the Victoria Institute, London, England, in Feb. 1947, on "The Present Status of Teleology." These subjects will be dealt with in one of the author's volumes on Christian Evidence.

with the philosopher Kant, that the power to distinguish between right and wrong is an inborn *human* characteristic: but this at best can only mean, as it does with Kant, that man by nature is able to make a *formal* distinction between right and wrong, not that he is able to make the *material* distinction. What he naturally counts right may be essentially wrong, and what he counts wrong may be essentially right." He may be conscious that there is good and evil, but he does not thereby know, without some other criteria, that this particular thing is really the thing that is evil or that is good. Although it may be true that he recognizes this in some instances, yet in the main he does not as is evidenced by the fact that men who really cut loose, in fact as well as theory, from faith in God soon hopelessly flounder as to the good and the evil; and often it simmers down just to what is pleasant or unpleasant, or what their repudiated religious background said was good or evil; when this is done he is sponging off of theism to get some standard by which to discredit theism. "There was probably a time," Lamont continues, "when all people thought it quite right to be cruel when circumstances called for cruelty. Where did the critic of Theism, then, get the criterion by which he condemns cruelty? Not from nature, not even from what is called natural evolution, but from faith, which however he does not share, that God is merciful. He has received his standard of moral judgment from Theism, though he is not aware of it. Having ascended by the theistic ladder, he now 'scorns the base degrees by which he did ascend.' That is a common error, but not a respectable one. We ought to agree, not only that Theism wrestles with the human difficulty at its decisive point, but that it also provides the human race with its standards of moral judgment."[3]

Not only are these questions in order, but the question ought also to be raised as to why—according to the unbelievers picture of the universe and life—man, in the face of the evil that there is in the world (which is sometimes overemphasized to the exclusion of the good in the world), ever "evolved" the idea of a good God?

---

[3]Lamont, *op. cit.*, pp. 167-168.

III. EVIL AND FREEDOM OF WILL

The account in the Bible of the entrance of evil into this world shows that death, and some of the present difficulties of man, entered into this world through sin. A curse was placed on the earth and man became subject to physical death. Belief, however, in the biblical account is a derived belief; that is, one believes it because he believes, on other grounds, that the Bible is the word of God. Thus it is that the believer is not overcome by the problem of evil, for he recognizes wherein it entered human life, since he has abundant grounds on which to believe that the Bible is the word of God. So to the unbeliever we say, study the basis of Christian faith and do not let the problem of evil keep you from seeing the reasons for faith.

The Christian believes that in so far as moral evil is concerned, the solution to that problem lies in the realm of the freedom of will. As long as God's mind was the only mind in the world there could be no problem of evil; but as soon as there were other minds, then there could be rebellion against the will of God. And thus it did come to pass that man chose to use his will contrary to God's will.

To illustrate more fully what is involved in man's freedom when it is abused, we shall briefly deal with the question which some ask: Why does not God step in and stop wars. Our suggestions, which follow, are not exhaustive, but they do indicate ways in which the question can be answered satisfactorily. First, God's will is that men walk in the paths of peace and love one another. This is clearly taught in the New Testament. Are we to blame God because men, who have the power of choice, will not listen to Him?

Second, when evil men persecute Christians, God may overrule it to the discipline and education of His people (Heb. 12:5; Rom. 5:3-5).

Third, God will not suspend the laws of the universe to keep us from being hurt if we ignore or rebel against these laws, and it is good that we cannot influence God to make us the exception. A man ultimately reaps what he sows (Gal. 6:7-8). If it were not so, life would be impossible both spiritually and physically for we would never know what produces what. If God made our will, rather than His the regulator of the universe, the universe would soon be wrecked, for the will of mankind is not united; instead there are millions of conflicting wills. Unless we could depend on the laws of nature, we could not plant a crop and know whether we were going to reap watermelons or grapefruit. This is not to say that God does not exercise any providence or answer prayer, but that it is His will which must be appealed to in all cases. We may entreat Him, but we cannot dictate to Him.

Fourth, for God to stop wars, to come back to our particular problem, one of two things must take place. (a) Either He must persuade all men through the gospel, and the leaven of the gospel, so that they become men of good will. (b) Or He must annihilate the will of man; thus annihilate humanity itself. The first thing is what God is now trying to do through the gospel, but because men have a will of their own, they must be persuaded, and thus Christ stands at the door and knocks (Rev. 3:20). He will not break the door down, we must open it. If God did the second thing, then He would have to remove the cause of war, which is sin in various forms. But God can remove that only through persuasion and our accepting of His gospel, or through removing the will of man. And if He removed the will of sinners or possible sinners, He would have to remove the will of all men, for all have sinned and fallen short of the glory of God. There is no one group of people entirely reponsible for the wars of the world; the sins of all make their contribution in varying degrees. And so then, for God to stop wars He would not stop eliminating men when He had eliminated all the Germans, etc., for in each man there is either greed, jealousy, and selfishness (which are at the root of war), or the possibility of these things. The process of annihilation of wills, and thus of personalities and the human being, would reach even unto me and to you.

Fifth, this world is a place of discipline and men must learn to be responsible for their own actions, for they shall reap as they have sown. To avoid reaping destruction, we must turn and sow to the Spirit.

Sixth, the world is also a place where righteous men often have to suffer because of the evil deeds of others. This fact is supremely demonstrated in the cross. We must accept it and recognize that the evil is in man's abuse of his power of choice, and that it may be given unto us to suffer for Christ's sake and if possible to reach the evil man and transform him, through the gospel, into a good man.

Seventh, in fairness to the Christian faith it must also be observed that the Bible teaches that although God may not always deliver Christian *from* death that He is able to deliver them *by* death. Death itself may be the means by which God permits them to be separated from their troubles and persecutions in this life, and to permit the spirit to return to God who gave it. Thus we conclude that even death itself is not the supreme problem to the Christian for he believes that life and immortality have been brought to light through the gospel of Jesus Christ (1 Tim. 1:12).

IN CONCLUSION

The problem of unbelief has not been dealt with intensively in these pages. Enough, however, has been said to indicate that the problem of evil need not keep an individual from accepting the credentials of Christianity. This problem he does not have to solve completely in order to have ample grounds for faith.

The interested reader is referred to a book on this subject by C. S. Lewis, *The Problem of Pain.*

CHAPTER XI

THE UNBELIEVER'S MISCONCEPTION OF EXPERIENCE

David Hume wrote a famous essay against miracles in which he argued that we know that testimony is frequently false; that a miracle is contrary to our experience; and that therefore any testimony to the effect that a miracle was performed by Jesus must be rejected. It is in harmony with our experience that testimony is often false, but it is not in harmony with our experience for miracles to happen; therefore, it is more likely that the testimony is false than that a miracle has actually taken place. Some have considered this to be an unanswerable argument against miracles as testified to by the New Testament. One of the excellent answers to this argument is found in the writings of Richard Whately. We shall present the gist of his answer.

I. THE TWOFOLD MEANING OF EXPERIENCE

Hume failed to distinguish between two different applications of the word *experience*. By *experience* we sometimes mean *general* experience and sometimes *our personal* experience, which is not based on the testimony or experience of another. If Hume had explained *"whose* Experience he meant, the argument would have come to nothing: if he means, the Experience of mankind universal, i. e. that a Miracle *has never* come under the Experience of *any one,* this is palpably begging the question: if he means the Experience of each individual who has never himself witnessed a Miracle, this would establish a rule (*viz.* that we are to believe nothing of which we have not ourselves experienced the like) which it would argue insanity to act upon. Not only was the King of Bantam justified (as Hume himself admits) in listening to no evidence for the existence of Ice, but *no one would be authorized on his principle to expect his own death.* His Experience informs him, directly, only that *others* have died. Every disease under which *he himself* may have labored, his Experience must have told him *has not* terminated fatally; if he is to judge strictly of the future by the past, according to this rule, what should hinder him from expecting the like of all future dieases?

"Perhaps however he meant, if indeed he had any distinct meaning, something intermediate between *universal,* and *individual* experience; *viz.* the Experience of the *generality,* as to what is common and of ordinary occurrence; in which sense the maxim will only amount to this, that false Testimony is a thing of common occurrence, and that Miracles are not. An obvious truth, indeed; but too general to authorize, of itself, a conclusion in any particular case. In any other individual question, as to the admissibility of evidence, it would be reckoned absurd to consider merely the *average chances* for the truth of *Testimony in the abstract,* without inquiring *what* the Testimony is, in the *particular instance* before us. As if e. g. any one had maintaned that no testimony could establish Columbus's account of the discovery of America, because it is more common for travelers to lie, than for new Continents to be discovered. Such a procedure involves a manifest ignoratic elenchi; the two propositions brought forward as opposed, being by no means incompatible: Experience tells us that 'a destructive hurricane is not a common occurrence'; certain persons tell us that 'a destructive hurricane occurred in the West Indies, at such a time'; there is (as Dr. Campbell has pointed out) no *opposition* between these two assertions.

"It is to be observed by the way, that there is yet an additional ambiguity in the *entire phrase* 'contrary to experience'; in one sense, a miracle, or any other event, may be *contrary* to the experience of any one who has never *witnessed* the like; as the freezing of water was to that of the King of Bantam; in another the stricter sense, that only is *contrary* to a man's experience, which he knows by experience not to be true; as if one should be told of an infallible remedy for some disorder, he having seen it administered without effect. No testimony can establish what is, *in this latter sense,* contrary to experience."

Not only do Hume's arguments reduce themselves to absurdity, when examined closely, but they also contradict other positions held by Hume. "The author himself seems plainly to have meant it as a specimen of his ingenuity in arguing on a given hypothesis; for he disputes against miracles as contrary to the Course of Nature; whereas, according to him, there is no such thing as a Course of Nature; his scepticism extends to the whole external world;—to every thing, except the ideas or impressions on the mind of the individual; so that a miracle which is *believed,* has, in that circumstance alone, on his principles a much reality as *any* thing *can* have."[1]

The answer Whately made to Hume is also the answer which can be made to the Pragmatist or Experimentalist today who rejects Christ and His wonders on the basis that the whole thing is contrary to experience.

II. The Myth of Hitler

The unbelievers, who argue against Christianity as did Hume, overlook the fact that their own arguments can be turned against them and used to disprove any other fact of history. The approach that some of them have used to deny that Jesus Christ ever existed can also be used to deny the existence of persons whose existence they have never thought to doubt and a doubt of which they would consider to be crazy. And yet, they must doubt the existence of these persons if they continue to cling to their so-called logic and follow it to its inevitable conclusion. Let us briefly use some of the arguments that skeptics have used to show that Christ is incredible, and apply them to the existence of Hitler.

I cannot admit the existence of Hitler for that such a person has ever lived is contrary to my experience. Neither I nor my friends have known of any character who has been able to do such amazing things with a whole nation. Our experience tells us that we have never met such a character; our experience also tells us that it is more likely that such a character should be a creation of fiction than of fact; therefore we cannot accept what newspapers and radios have told us about Hitler.

Of course, we realize that newspapers have played up the fiction of Hitler but that does not prove his existence. It is well

---

[1]Richard Whately, *Elements of Logic,* Boston: James Munroe and Co., 1854. 9th Edition. pp. 333-335

known that many men are greedy and will do anything for money. Newspapers will play up those things which increase their sales. Our experience has shown us countless instances wherein men have deceived others for money; but our experience has never embraced a Hitler. Therefore, it is much more likely that newspapers have perpetuated a fraud than that such a one as Hitler ever existed.

Do you object that not only our newspapers but the papers of Germany have testified to his existence. That is easily accounted for. Nations are composed of men and women. The vanity of men and women is well known. People tell things which will magnify their class, race or nation for the bigger the heroes of their nation the more that they feel that they themselves are elevated. Nations tend to exhalt themselves by building up myths of national heroes. Not only do myths tend to thus exalt them in their own eyes, and in the eyes of other nations, but they are also helpful in bringing pressure to bear on other nations to get them to do the will of your nation. And if you can threaten them with persons like Hitler, they will fall the more readily through fear of your nation.

Perhaps you saw a picture of Hitler. All that we need to say is that pictures may not lie but liars will take pictures and label them in such a way as to suit their purposes. How do you know that the picture which you saw was Hitler? Even the Germans admitted that he had a double. And even if it was someone called Hitler, how could you prove that the one in the picture had done all the amazing things with the Germans and with Europe which they have claimed that he did?

Or did you see some reporter who claimed to have met Hitler? Perhaps he was deceived by being ushered into the presence of someone whom they called Hitler? But how could he prove that the person whom he had met had done all of the things attributed to Hitler? It could be that the censors would not let the reporter send any other mesage through. Furthermore, one must not overlook the possibility that, since liars are more common than even the myths of such persons as Hitler, it is more likely that the reporter is lying in order to have a good story with which to make money.

We also point out that there are some books which do not mention Hitler and which were written in Germany during the time when the myths tell us of Hitler's existence. Surely if Hitler had lived, he would have been such an amazing character that no author would have dared to have left him unmentioned. Surely all writers would have *known* of his existence and they would have *mentioned* it. Since all do not mention it, that is sufficient proof that he did not exist.

Word has come through the newspapers that Hitler is dead. Surely this confirms us in our belief that he was never anything but a myth by means of which the German people tried to magnify the glory of their own nation. As soon as people really began to try to find out whether there was a Hitler, in order to bring him to trial, it was a most convenient thing to say that he was dead. Our suspicion is strengthened in that they also say that his body has disappeared! Surely we can all see through such a hoax.

Perhaps the reader is ready to say that this is sheer mockery; that there was a Hitler and that he was one of the causes of the death of many fine people. That is all true. But we ask the reader to remember what a mockery it is to claim that Jesus Christ, who has saved millions, never existed or that he is the product of a group of stories which grew up around a mere man. The absurd-ities which we have suggested with reference to Hitler are not only absurdities with reference to the conclusions themselves, but also absurdities which are bound up in the logic which some have used to deny the claims of Christ, and to reach such conclusions.

If the reader is interested in an extensive treatment of the "existence" of another figure of history, Napoleon, according to the principles of Hume, let him consult Richard Whately's *His-toric Doubts Relative to Napoleon Bonaparte.*

Chapter XII

YOUTH AND UNBELIEF

It is common knowledge that there are many young people who experience a fierce conflict between faith and unbelief. In this struggle some succumb. In many cases, they lose their faith while in college. Why is this so? And what can be done to deal with the problem and to keep faith in college? It is due in a large measure to the fact that children pass from the place of dependency on their parents to a period of questioning which involves an effort to stand on their own feet. This period can be dealt with so that disaster does not finally result if the situation is rightly understood and correctly approached. Let us first consider unbelief as related to the transition which takes place in the life of the adolescent as he endeavors to think for himself. Then let us see how one can keep faith in college.

I. The Age of Self-Assertion and Unbelief

The boys and girls finally reach the age when they more and more assert their own personality. They begin to stand on their own feet and think for themselves. This is commendable and necessary, but it is also a time which demands a great deal of wise understanding on the part of the parents. It also means that before this time arrives parents by word and example must have instilled into the character and habits of the child those principles which will act as stabilizing influences and which although they may swing away from them for a time, will help bring them back to an even keel. The parents who have been in the confidence of their children are the ones who, during this period of the struggle for independence, will be the ones who are given by the children access to their problems and thus opportunities to guide—not dictate—them.

It is at this age that many individuals begin to feel that their parents have been dominating them and that they are somewhat old fashion and behind the times. It is told of Mark Twain that when he was entering this period that he was surprised at how dumb his daddy was, but that within a few years he was amazed at how much his dad had learned. In other words, he had passed through the period in which he felt that his parent was somewhat behind the times, and later had entered into the one where he recognized how little he knew and that after all his dad knew a great many things. The adolescent is also passing through a period in which restraint becomes more and more irksome and seems less and less reasonable. For that reason they often rebel against the authority of the parents. "If parents are wise enough to sense the need for reasonable readjustment of authority at this period, serious consequences are averted." They must recognize that more and more the child must stand on his own, and that they must give assistance that will help him in doing so, not that will hinder and arouse his resentment.

"The next line of defenses which are attacked are those of religious authority. For religion is a real regulative power in the life of a child. Here, however, open revolt does not accomplish the desired object. For one's own conscience is such a large factor in the problem that some other tactics must be adopted. It is for this reason that the subtle strategy of psychological camouflage is employed. While the problem is distinctly psychological, yet the intellectual difficulties which the progress of modern science and Biblical criticism have created, furnish a most convenient excuse for rejecting the authority of religion. If to the assertion: 'I do not think everything wrong you and father do,' is added: 'I do not believe everything you and father do,' the childhood defenses of home and Church are shattered. And the external authority which might have suppressed the growing individuality of the child is forced to allow this new personality to become a cooperator in making and exercising voluntary control.

"Up to this point, however, the young are only feigning intellectual unbelief. Genuine intellectual difficulties which strike deep down to the very roots of their religious faith are still unknown. Their real problems are moral and spiritual, and they know this perfectly well all the while they are trying to camouflage this fact by throwing up a barrage of intellectual difficulties between them and their elders. Genuine intellectual difficulties are rare among uneducated adolescents. They do not develop sufficient interest in the intellectual probems involved to make that phase of the problem of any vital importance. This is the reason they enjoy shocking their elders with their new ideas and denials. As soon as the religious worker understands this truth, it is a simple matter to dig down and find out the psychological trouble which is masquerading in the garb of intellectual unbelief. Little serious attention need be paid to the religious doubts and denials of this group of adolescents. For theirs is really pseudo-unbelief or rationalization." Wyckoff, of course, does not mean that one should not point out to them the peculiar fallacies which underline the criticisms of religion which they have heard elsewhere and pass on to the adult. But he means that one should recognize that there are problems of adjustment beneath this brazen exterior; problems which need wise, patient attention; and which must be looked for beyond the bare statements of the young person.

This stage of unbelief, however, can develop into something very serious if the child is constantly exposed to an atmosphere which is anti-christian and which endeavors to drill into the student intellectual reasons for unbelief. In many colleges this takes place. The child is no longer under the influence of the home which gives attention to his religious life, but is placed in an atmosphere where even when religion is not opposed, in various subtle ways, at least it is not encouraged and opportunities for spiritual growth are neither required nor made available in the general environment that is maintained by the college itself. The professors occupy high positions of authority in the minds of the students and they may hang on every word as a "thus saith the Lord." The material that is presented in class lectures may be presented with an anti-christian bias, for the biases of such teachers will come out in their lectures as well as in the material which they require the student to read—the textbook and other assigned readings. The student has to study these things, for he must meet material on tests which are taken out of these readings. And thus while the spiritual life is receiving little or no attention, or food, the anti-spiritual is receiving a great deal of attention and food;

and what we feed ourselves intellectually we think on; and as a man thinketh in his heart so is he.

The material presented to students, who are passing through this period of reaction against restraint, may be such as to state definitely that the facts are against religion; when in reality all that is against it is not the facts, but the devilish, blind, bias, of some unfair college professor who makes ex cathedra statements in such a way as to mislead the student. For example: "When Professor Leuba sums up the theological situation in these words: 'Theism having become logically impossible and pantheism being practically insufficient, where shall we look for a religion of the future?' he is serving up the unripe fruits of scholarship to his students. When such statements as the above are heard in the class room or read in his book on *A Psychological Study of Religion* (see page 321), the impression is given that to the informed, theism has 'become logically impossible' as a tenet of reason and faith. But what right has a college professor to inculcate that idea in the mind of the student? The verdict of scholarship and science has not yet been rendered in favor of atheism. And it is farther from favouring that theory than it was at the beginning of the century. A statement such as Professor Leuba makes above, might be justified in the company of his colleagues and peers, who are in position to weigh its evidence, and defend their religious beliefs; but immature adolescents have no defense against such generalizations."[2] Especially when the student is in an unsettled and impressionable age, and when the platform of the professor is surrounded with all the "halo" for him that once surrounded the pulpit of the preacher when the student was younger. Men of the type who do such things are far worse enemies to the welfare of humanity, to its social and moral progress, than gangsters. People as a whole know that the gangster is wrong, but the professor of the above type is supposed to represent scholarship, and an unbiased attitude. Furthermore, the attitude of the relativity of morality which some of these professors inculcate justifies in reality, although they may deny it, the moral code of the gangster. Proof of this state-

---

[2]Professor Albert Clarke Wyckoff, *Acute and Chronic Unbelief*. New York: Fleming H. Revell Company, 1924, pp. 16, 17, 22, 23.

ment will be advanced in the book, to be published by the author
the Lord willing, on *Christianity's Challenge to Pragmatism* and in
The Faith and Fruits of Atheism.

In order further to elaborate and illustrate the point under
consideration Wyckoff put in this way: "Doubt is the natural
intellectual hunger of the healthy-minded adolescent. (He is beginning to think for himself and thus to question some of the
things which he has been told in times past, J. D. B.) The inter-
rogation point is the hand that beckons the hungry mind to the
banqueting hall where modern thinking has spread a most bounti-
ful and appetizing feast of good things. It is not to be wondered
at if the hungry mind of the modern adolescent prefers these
new, freshly prepared viands of the present, to the cold, or
warmed-over left-overs of the intellectual feasts of our fathers.
All this they may be allowed to enjoy, without having their doubts
nourished into positive unbelief. It is only when abnormally
stimulated by certain intellectual ideas that adolescent doubt
develops into positive unbelief. For psychology has clearly proven
that this same adolescent period is the period of conversion. Doubt
is a peculiar mental, chemical solvent that has the power to soften
beliefs and ideas so that they are capable of being remoulded.
When in this plastic condition it is not a difficult task to remould
such beliefs and ideas into useful beliefs, or into unbelief. And
the college professor, who has the adolescent under his teaching in
the classroom for several hours a day for five days a week, with
the demands of examinations and tests thrown in, has the very
best opportunity in the world to remould the beliefs doubt has
softened, according to his will. And no preacher or religious
teacher or parent, having only an occasional touch with the adolescent and no regular intellectual authority over attention, can com-
pete against such an advantage. The Roman Catholic Church realizes that this is too precious an opportunity to take any chances
on, so it turns its adolescents over to its trained religious teachers.
It would be well if Protestants began to realize why unbelief is
becoming epidemic among college students."[3]

---

[3]*Ibid.,* pp. 24-25.

These considerations lead us to the next question: *How can faith be kept in college?* Of course, the principles which enable one to keep faith in college will enable him to keep faith else-where. Since, however, so many of the probems of faith and the causes of unbelief operate during the college days the problem is being considered with special reference to keeping faith in college.

II. KEEPING FAITH IN COLLEGE

"I wonder now an intelligent man like you can believe the Bible," remarked a well known Professor, who had shown me many kindness, just after my Ph. D. dissertation had been accepted by my committee. This turned my attention again to the fact that although some people lose faith in the time of their University life, my faith had grown stronger. Why was it so? Why did some lose faith in college, and how was it possible to keep faith during graduate as well as undergraduate years. Of course, I had had a favorable start for my undergraduate work had been done in Harding College where the Bible is adhered to as God's inspired word. Christians should attend such schools for at least part of their college work. This gives one a good start. For several years, however, I had done graduate work in secular schools and in some cases I had had professors who were not only unbelievers but who also made efforts, in one way or another, to shake the faith of believing students. This, I am glad to say, was not the case with the Professor who asked the question which introduced this paragraph. Let us now consider some reasons why some lose faith in college and why others experience a growth of faith under the same type of school influence, but who in reality *live* in a different environment.

III. LOSING FAITH VS. KEEPING FAITH

Environment, not argument. Many times persons experience a loss of faith not because of the arguments which are brought against faith, but because one eats and breathes, so to speak, in a secular atmosphere. The spiritual man is just as much in need of spiritual food and exercise as the physical man is in need of food and exercise. One can become unhealthy through receiving false teaching concerning health and being thus lead into dissipation. He may be convinced by arguments that certain practices are not harmful when in reality they are very harmful. On the other hand, he may not be convinced by the arguments and yet he may lose his health because he fails to eat proper food, negects physical exercise, and does not take the proper steps to guard against disease. Just so, the arguments of an unbeliever may not be very powerful, but if a believer neglects spiritual food and exercise, the spiritual man becomes weaker and weaker and may finally show no signs of life.

Another factor in the environment is that the pressing duties of college work may be permitted to crowd out Bible study, prayer, and Christian association. As a man thinketh in his heart so is he. And if a man studies only secular subjects and fills his head and heart with these things only, he thinks only upon these things, and thus he does not become spiritual. He ceases to pray, and prayer is essential to the life of the soul. He neglects the assembly of the saints and thus misses the spiritual benefits of Christian fellowship and worship. He runs with a worldly group and thus is influenced by their outlook on life. If a person expects to stay alive spiritually, he must do at least the following: *First,* he must study the Bible. He can find time for this even if he has to take some time from his other studies. Set aside some time each day for Bible study and let nothing keep you from such study. You will have to put it in your daily schedule, or you will not "find" time for it. One must feed on the word of God. He cannot live by bread alone, and to try to do so is to invite disaster. *Second,* he must work for Christ. Do not regard your college life as a vacation from Christian duties. Think of how you can serve Christ in college. Contact others of like mind and arrange for a meeting at least once during the week. Colleges will often let you have a room for such purposes. Some of the group may take part in the leadership of the class, and outside speakers may also be invited in to help you deal with your problems. Arrange some time to visit the sick and to help the needy. Without actual practice of the principles of Christianity, they tend to become merely verbal statements of doctrines which bear no living relationship to life. Because they are merely verbal, they do not have the ring of reality; they are vague and lifeless, and thus one finally gives them up because they seem unreal. If, on the other hand, one had actually practiced these principles, he would have experienced the fact that they are alive; that they have the ring of reality; and thus they would have become a part of him, and he would not have lost faith in them. *Third,* attend church services, including Bible classes, Sunday morning and Sunday night. Also, Wednesday night, or whatever night they have their midweek service. Plan to do this every week, and then attend whatever other gatherings of Christians you have an opportunity to attend. But above all, do not neglect the above services. Worship and Christian fellowship are absolutely essential to a continuation of spiritual life, and you neglect them at the peril of *your* soul. Do not attend a college where you will be entirely cut off from Christian fellowship. If there is no congregation in the town where you attend college, advertise in the paper for contacts with other members, and start a congregation. If you are unable to do this, attend the nearest congregation, or go elsewhere to college. In fact, find out about the church before you go and look up brethren as soon as you get there. Don't put it off; delay may result in a drift into apostasy. *Fourth,* make prayer a part of your life. Pray not only at stated intervals, but whenever you feel the need for it; even while walking across the campus one may breathe a prayer to God; or when faced with difficulties in the class room. Any time is prayer time. *Fifth,* associate with Christian boys and girls in college. It is not always possible to find them, and when you cannot find them in the same college with you, at least seek out spiritually minded boys and girls with whom to associate.

Some people lose faith in college *because they go to college with the wrong purpose in mind.* They want to become educated in order to make a name for themselves or to enable them to make a lot of money for selfish purposes. Such people, of course, will neglect the spiritual things in life and follow after those things which will bring selfish advancement. Because they have the wrong motive, they are headed in the wrong direction, in the way which leads to spiritual impoverishment and death. It is right to want an education. But the question is: For what purpose do you want it?

An educated person can serve God and humanity. An uneducated one can too, for that matter. The more one knows, however, and the more one can do, and the larger may be one's opportunities for service; if one is willing to dedicate what he is and has to God and the service and salvation of mankind. Some uneducated persons, in so far as the world views education, may in reality be far better educated spiritually, and with reference to service and the true meaning of life, than some who have attained high honors in secular education. One is not uneducated if he knows God and His will, although he may not have a degree from a secular institution. A person who is educated in heart and spirit will also want to take advantage of whatever opportunities he can make to be educated along other lines. And he should do so with the purpose of becoming an even better instrument in the hand of God. What is your purpose in seeking an education?

There are some who do not lose faith in college, but who find out while in college that they never had much faith. They simply had a second-hand faith. They were brought up in a religious environment, but they never really became religious. They were imitators, with reference to the spiritual life, rather than participators. They went through the forms of Christianity because others were going through these forms. They never made a personal decision for Christ. They never walked by faith, but by imitation. They copied, but they did not capture spiritual life. Therefore, when they went into a secular environment, they discovered that they did not have any spiritual foundations. They then began to imitate those around them in colleges as they had once imitated those who were around them when they were in a religious atmosphere. A person must not only have facts and forms, but he must also have faith.

There are some who stand in such awe of their college professors that they take their word, without any other evidence or support, as the truth, regardless of what they may say. I do not discourage respect for one's teachers or for true scholarship. And yet, the teacher is just a human being, a fallible one, regardless of how many degrees he may possess. He is subject to the same prejudices to which others are subjected. He may be a famous scientist, but he may not have an open mind. I know of one professor who wanted to flunk a student, who was in a history class, because the student disagreed with the professor on the theory of organic evolution. A professor is not a god, he is just a man, therefore do not accept his word as infallible. He may be very well versed in his field, but in spite of his scholarly attainments, one must remember at least two things. *First,* his scholarship in one field does not make him an authority in another field. He may know a great deal about bugs and nothing about bugles. And yet, because he is an expert "Bug-ologist" a student may think that he is an authority in religion. He may have never read the Bible or anything that is favorable to it. He may not be as much of an authority on the Bible as a five year old child in a religious home. Therefore, one should not "let" his authority as a "bug-ologist" transfer to religion and make him an authority there. He may have a "halo" and authority when talking about bugs, but "horns" and prejudice when talking about religion. *Second,* there is a difference between facts which the professor may know and the interpretations which he places on them. The facts are one thing and his theory, with which he attempts to unify and explain the facts, is another thing. Thus though he may be an authority with reference to the facts, he is not necessarily one with reference to the theories. There are some professors who will tell you when they have left the realm of facts and when they have started with their theories. There are others who will not do so. Perhaps, they do not know themselves. Perhaps, they never thought about it. But as a student, you will find it necessary to distinguish between the facts and the interpretations. You may accept his facts, without accepting his theories.

There are some who cannot stand up in the face of *ridicule.* In a secular institution on the west coast one professor carried on a dialogue in which he represented the believer as saying that he was afraid to study biology least it wreck his faith. The believer was thus placed in a ridiculous position. The writer has seen students laughed at when they made some statement which indicated their faith in God or the Bible. Some are unwilling to stand ridicule and thus they abandon their faith.

Some have been frightened out of their weak faith by the belligerent cocksureness of some unbelievers. Some college students are overawed by unbelieving professors. These may talk and act as if Christianity is so blatantly false, that only a fool would believe it. It is assumed that although once it was possible to believe that now it is impossible. The impression is left on the mind of some timid believers that never before has the Bible been attacked; and that since unbelievers are so certain that at last it has been overthrown perhaps the Bible will be unable to survive the attack.

It should be clearly recognized that the Bible has been under attack long before our generation. In fact it has always been attack by some person, even when it was being spoken—before being written—by God's prophets of old. The central theme of the Bible, Jesus Christ, was under attack in His lifetime and they placed Him on the cross, but they did not do away with Him. Just so with His word, it has been under attack but after each fierce encounter it shines brighter than before. In order that young people might recognize that unbelievers have assured the world in centuries past that the Bible was now demolished, the following quotations are presented. The first is from the pen of Joseph Butler and was written in 1736. "It is come, I know not how, to be taken for granted, by many persons, that Christianity is not so much as a subject inquiry; but that it is, now at length, discovered to be fictitious. And accordingly they treat it, as if, in the present age, this was an agreed point among people of discernment; and nothing remained, but to set it up as a principal subject of mirth and ridicule, as it were by way of reprisals, for its having so long interrupted the pleasures of the world. On the contrary, thus much, at least, will be here found, not taken for granted, but proved, that any reasonable man, who will thoroughly consider the matter, may be as much assured, as he is of his own being, that it is not, however, so clear a case, that there is nothing in it. There is, I think, strong evidence of its truth; but it is certain no one can, upon principles of reason, be satisfied of the contrary. And the practical consequence to be drawn from this, is not attended to, by everyone who is concerned in it."[4]

"Burnet tells that about the year 1700 it became a common topic to treat all mysteries in religion as the contrivance of priests, and 'priestcraft' came into fashion as a term of derision. Dean Swift, in 1708, dwells upon the rapidity with which freethinking ideas had spread from the upper classes to the body of the people. It was commonly held, he said that the system of the Gospel had become antiquated and exploded, after the fate of other systems, the common folks having grown ashamed of it, as their betters had done before. Still later, in 1754, it was publicly suggested that the churches should be turned into freethinking meetinghouses, and a new liturgy compiled, opposite to our present one, and that instead of lessons being taken from the Bible, they should consist of extracts from the works of the Deists."[5]

H. A. Taine, in *The Ancient Regime* wrote as follows concerning 18th century France. "A little while ago some one put this question to one of the most respectable curates in Paris: Do you think that the bishops who insist so strenuously on religion have much of it themselves? The worthy pastor replied, after a moment's hestitation: 'There may be four or five among them who still believe.' "[6] Some of that generation predicted that the Bible would soon be only a museum piece, but today it is still the world's best seller. The Bible wears out its critics instead of being worn out by them.

> "Last eve I passed beside a blacksmith's door
>   And heard the anvil ring the vesper chime;
> When looking it, I saw upon the floor,
>   Old hammers worn with beating years of time.
>
> 'How many anvils have you had,' said I,
>   "To wear and batter all these hammers so?"
> 'Just one,' said he; then said with twinkling eye,
>   "The anvil wears the hammers out you know.'

---

[4]*The Analogy of Religion*, 30th Edition, 1858, pp. 28-29.
[5]John Langtry, *A Struggle for Life*, pp. 38-39.
[6]p. 293.

And so, I thought, the anvil of God's word
    For ages skeptic's blows have beat upon;
Yet, though the noise of falling blows was heard
    The anvil unharmed—the hammers gone!"

—Anonymous

And so we say to the timid believer, be not afraid of the noise made by some unbelievers. The Bible has stood the test of time and of every form of attack and its voice will be heard long after that of the unbeliever has been silenced.

CHAPTER XIII

A PERSONAL WORD WITH THE UNBELIEVER

The author cannot conclude this book without expressing his deep concern for those who do not accept the gospel of Jesus Christ. For them, as well as for Christians, this book has been written in order to help them better approach the credentials of Christianity. If you do not believe the Bible will you please sincerely face the following questions. *First,* have I really considered the evidence of Christianity, or have I simply spent my time hunting up objections and dealing with the fringe of the field of Christian evidence? *Second,* would I be willing to undergo a complete change of life—in so far as my life is out of harmony with Christianity—it I conclude that the Bible is true? *Third,* have I allowed wrong methods and attitudes to keep me from fairly evaluating the evidence? *Fourth,* have I simply been indifferent to its evidence, and even somewhat afraid to examine th Bible? *Fifth,* would I reject something else—if it did not make a demand that my way of life be changed—that had as much for it as there is for the Bible?

I. THERE IS MUCH AT STAKE

There is much at stake. If the Christian is right the unbeliever is in a terrible condition. If the Christian is wrong, and the unbeliever right, the Christian has lived a more hopeful, and happy, life here and he will never know that he was wrong. If the unbeliever is wrong he will always know it and he has lost the best in this life as well as in the life to come. The things which are at stake are so tremendous that one ought to study them far more diligently than he would study a claim which might place him in line to inherit billions. These considerations alone should spur the unbeliever on to study seriously the credentials of Christ. If the author can help you he shall be happy to do so.

II. Face the Real Issue

The unbeliever is urged to face the real issue. and not false ones. This book has shown that wrong conclusions are drawn; misleading questions are raised; evidence is never seen or if seen is not really evaluated; because people do not see the real issue. The real issue is not whether any *objections* can be raised for objections can be raised concerning anything. It is not whether some *questions* are unanswerable, for some questions are un-answerable concerning any fact of history. The real issue is not whether there are *mysteries*—things that human reason cannot fathom—in the Bible; all life has its mysteries and yet life is not for that reason rejected. The true issue is not whether there are Christians whose life falls below their confession. *The issue is whether or not there is sufficient evidence to justify the belief that the Bible is the word of God—that it was written by super-human power—and whether Jesus is what He claimed to be.*

III. Study the Bible Itself

One of the essential things in facing the real issue is to study the Bible. This includes more than merely picking it up; glancing at it; being puzzled by some passage; and closing it. Study it closely and study also some of the books which have been mentioned in this book.

One of the reasons that one should study the Bible is that much of the evidence of the truthfulness of the Bible is found in the Bible itself. As one would expect from a book of which God is the real author, it has certain self-evidencing power. Furth-ermore, there is a general impression of the truthfulness of the Bible which one gains by reading it, and can gain in no other way. It is sometimes difficult to put into words certain types of evidence. There are some things which, if they are not evident to the one who examines them, are difficult to formulate as ab-stract arguments. If, for example, a man cannot see for himself the vast difference between man and the animals, between a hu-man being a mere animal, it would be very difficult to prove it to him. Dr. Paley well wrote, in *Horae Paulinae,* that "When we take into our hands the letters," of Paul, "which the suffrage and consent of antiquity hath thus transmitted to us, the first thing that strikes our attention is the air of reality and business, as well as of seriousness and conviction, which pervades the whole. Let the sceptic read them. If he be not sensible of these qualities in them, the argument can have no weight with him. If he be; if he perceive in almost every page the language of a mind actuated by real occasions, and operating upon real circumstances; I would wish it to be observed, that the proof which arises from this perception is not to be deemed occult or imaginary, because it is incapable of being drawn out in words, or of being conveyed to the apprehension of the reader in any other way, than by sending him to the books themselves."[7] This is one of the reasons that we urge unbelievers to study the Bible itself in weighing the evidence of Christianity. It contains evidences and arguments which are difficult to put otherwise than they are put therein. This type of evidence may have struck home to the believer, but he may not be able to explain it to the unbeliever, who fails to read the Bible itself. As Whately said: "In all subjects indeed, persons unaccustomed to writing or discussion, but possessing natural sagacity, and experience in particular departments, have been observed to be generally unable to give a satisfactory reason for their judgments, even on points on which they are actually very good judges (See Aristotle's Ethics, B.vi). This is a defect which it is the business of education (especially the present branch of it) to surmount or diminish. After all, however, in some subjects, no language can adequately convey (to the inexperienced at least) all the indications which influence the judgment of an acute and practised observer."[8]

This is one type of evidence which has often impressed the believer who has made a thorough study of the Bible; but has not done it from the standpoint of searching for material for reasoning on the subject of Christian evidence with an unbeliever. Thus when asked by an unbeliever for reasons for the hope which

---

[7]Quoted by Richard Whately, *Elements of Rhetoric*, New York: Harper and Brothers, Publishers, 1860, pp. 86-87.
[8]*Ibid.*, p. 88.

is within him, he may not always be able to formulate this type of evidence and present it to the unbeliever. The unbeliever may conclude that the person has no ground for his faith, although he may have a great many reasons for it. Not all, of course, of Christian evidence is of this nature, but some of it is and this aspect of it will never be seen by the unbeliever unless he is willing to study seriously the Bible itself.

Friend, what stands between you and faith in Christ?

APPENDIX

"OF THE SUPPOSED DEFICIENCY IN THE PROOF OF REVELATION"

First, The evidence of religion not appearing obvious, may constitute one particular part of some men's trial in the religious sense; as it gives scope for a virtuous exercise, or vicious neglect, of their understanding, in examining or not examining into that evidence. There seems no possible reason to be given, why we may not be in a state of moral probation with regard to the exercise of our understanding upon the subject of religion, as we are with regard to our behaviour in common affairs. The former is as much a thing within our power and choice as the latter. And I suppose it is to be laid down for certain, that the same character, the same inward principle which, after a man is convinced of the truth of religion, renders him obedient to the precepts of it, would, were he not thus convinced, set him about an examination of it, upon its system and evidence being offered to his thoughts; and that, in the latter state, his examina-tion would be with an impartiality, seriousness, and solicitude proportionable to what his obedience is in the former. And as inattention, negligence, want of all serious concern about a mat-ter of such a nature and such importance, when offered to men's consideration is, before a distinct conviction of its truth, as real immoral depravity and dissoluteness, as neglect of religious prac-tice after such conviction; so active solictude about it, and fair impartial consideration of its evidence before such conviction, is as really an exercise of a morally right temper, as is religious practice after. Thus, that religion is not intuitively true, but a matter of deduction and inference; that a conviction of its truth is not forced upon every one, but left to be, by some, collected with heedful attention to premises: this as much constitutes

---

[1] Bishop Butler, Analogy of Religion, New York: Harper and Brothers, 1854, pp. 264-271.

religious probation, as much affords sphere, scope, opportunity, for right and wrong behaviour, as any thing whatever does: and their manner of treating this subject, when laid before them, shows what is in their heart, and is an exertion of it.

Secondly, It appears to be a thing as evident, though it is not so much attended to, that if, upon consideration of religion, the evidence of it should seem to any persons doubtful, in the highest supposable degree, even this doubtful evidence will, however, put them into a *general state of probation* in the moral and religious sense. For suppose a man to be really in doubt, whether such a person had not done him the greatest favour; or whether his whole temporal interest did not depend upon that person; no one, who had any sense of gratitude and of prudence, could possibly consider himself in the same situation, with regard to such person, as if he had no such doubt. In truth, it is as just to say, that certainty and doubt are the same, as to say, the situations now mentioned would leave a man as entirely at liberty, in point of gratitude or prudence, as he would be, were he certain he had received no favour from such person, or that he no way depended upon him. And thus, though the evidence of religion which is afforded to some men, should be little more than that they are given to see the system of Christianity, or religion in general, to be supposable and credible, this ought in all reason to beget serious practical apprehension that it may be true. And even this will afford matter of exercise for religious suspense and deliberation, for moral resolution and self-government; because the apprehension that religion may be true, does as really lay men under obligations, as a full conviction that it is true: It gives occasion and motives to consider farther the important subject; to preserve attentively upon their minds a general implict sense that they may be under divine moral government; an awful solicitude about religion, whether natural or revealed. Such apprehension ought to turn men's eyes to every degree of new light which may be had, from whatever side it comes, and induce them to refrain, in the meantime, from all immoralities, and live in the conscientious practice of every common virtue. Especially are they bound to keep at the greatest distance from all dissolute profaneness; for this the very nature of the case forbids; and to treat with highest reverence a matter upon which their own whole interest and being, and the fate of nature, depend. This behavior, and an active endeavour to maintain within themselves this temper, is the business, the duty, and the wisdom of those persons who complain of the doubtful-ness of religion; is what they are under the most proper obliga-tions to; and such behavior is an exertion of, and has a tend-ency to improve in them, that character, which the practice of all the several duties of religion, from a full conviction of its truth, is an exertion of, and has a tendency to improve in others —others I say, to whom God has afforded such conviction (through an examination of the very evidence with which they are now being made acquainted, J. D. B.) Nay, considering the infinite importance of religion, revealed as well as natural, I think it may be said in general, that whoever will weigh the matter thoroughly, may see there is not near so much difference, as is commonly imagined, between what ought in reason to be the rule of life, to those persons who are fully convinced of its truth, and to those who have only a serious doubting apprehension that it may be true. Their hopes, and fears, and obligations, will be in various degrees; but, as the subject-matter of their hopes and fears is the same, so the subject-matter of their obligations, what they are bound to do and to refrain from, is not so very unlike.

"It is to be observed, farther, that from a character of un-derstanding, or a situation of influence in the world, some per-sons have it in their power to do infinitely more harm or good, by setting an example of profaneness and avowed disregard to all religion, or, on the contrary, of a serious though, perhaps, doubt-ing apprehension of its truth, and of a reverent regard to it under this doubtfulness, than they can do by acting well or ill in all the common intercourses amongst mankind; and, con-sequently, they are most highly accountable for a behaviour which, they may easily foresee, is of such importance, and in which there is most plainly a right and a wrong; even admitting the evidence of religion to be as doubtful as is pretended.

"The ground of these observations, and that which renders them just and true, is, that doubting necessarily implies some degree of evidence for that of which we doubt. For no person would be in doubt concerning the truth of a number of facts so and so circumstanced, which should accidentally come into his thoughts, and of which he had no evidence at all. And though in the case of an even chance, and where consequently we were in doubt, we should in common language say, that we have no evidence at all for either side; yet that situation of things which renders it an even chance, and no more, that such an event will happen, renders this case equivalent to all others, where there is such evidence on both sides of a question as leaves the mind in doubt concerning the truth. Indeed, in all these cases, there is no more evidence on the one side than on the other; but there is (what is equivalent to) much more for either, than the truth of a number of facts which come into ones thoughts at random. And thus, in all these cases, doubt as much presupposes evidence, lower degrees of evidences, as belief presupposes higher, and certainty higher still. Any one, who will a little attend to the nature of evidence, will easily carry this observation on, and see, that between no evidence at all, and that degree in which affords ground of doubt, there are as many intermediate degrees, as there are between that degree which is the ground of doubt and demonstration. And, though we have not faculties to distinguish these degrees of evidence with any sort of exactness, yet, in proportion as they are discerned, they ought to influence our practice; for it is as real an imperfection on the moral character, not to be influenced in practice by a lower degree of evidence when discerned, as it is in the understanding not to discern it. And as, in all subjects which men consider, they discern the lower as well as higher degrees of evidence, proportionably to their capacity of understanding; so in practicable subjects, they are influenced in practice by the lower as well as higher degrees of it, proportionably to their fairness and honesty. And as of evidence, are in danger of overlooking evidence when it is not glaring, and are easily imposed upon in such cases; so, in proportion to the corruption of the heart, they seem capable of satisfying themselves with having no regard to practice to evidence acknowledged real, if it be not overbearing. From these things it must follow, that doubt concerning religion implies such a degree of evidence for it, as joined with the consideration of its importance, unquestionably lays men under the obligations before mentioned, to have a dutiful regard to it in all their behavior.

Thirdly, The difficulties in which the evidence of religion is inolved, which some complain of, is no more a just ground of complaint, than the external circumstances of temptation, which others are placed in; or than difficulties in the practice of it, after a full conviction of its truth. Temptations render our state a more improving state of discipline, than it would be otherwise; as they give occasion for a more attentive exercise of the virtuous principle, which confirms and strengthens it more than an easier or less attentive exercise of it could. Now speculative difficulties are, in this respect, of the very same nature with these external temptations. For the evidence of religion not appearing obvious, is to some persons a temptation to reject it, without any consideration at all; and therefore requires such an attentive exercise of the virtuous principle, seriously to consider that evidence, as there would be no occasion for, but for such temptation. And the supposed doubtfulness of its evidence, after it has been in some sort considered, affords opportunity to an unfair mind, of explaining away, and deceitfully hiding from itself, that evidence which it might see: and also for men's encouraging themselves in vice, from hopes of impunity, though they do clearly see thus much at least, that these hopes are uncertain: in like manner as the common temptation to many instances of folly, which end in temporal infamy and ruin, is the ground for hope of not being detected, and of escaping with impunity; i.e. the doubtfulness of the proof beforehand, that such foolish behaviour will thus end in infamy and ruin. On the contrary, supposed doubtfulness in the evidence of religion calls for a more careful and attentive exercise of the virtuous principle, in fairly yielding themselves up to the proper influences of any real evidence, though doubtful; and in practising conscientiously all virtue, though under some uncertainty, whether the government in the universe may not possibly be such, as that vice may escape with impunity. And in general, temptation, meaning by this word the lesser allurements to wrong, and difficulties in the discharge of our duty, as well as the greater ones; temptation, I say, as such and of every kind and degree, as it calls forth some virtuous efforts, additional to what would otherwise have been wanting, cannot but be an additional discipline and improvement of virtue, as well as probation of it, in the other senses of that word. So that the very same account is to be given, why the evidence of religion should be left in such a manner, as to require, in some, an attentive, solicitous, perhaps painful, exercise of their understanding about it; as why others should be placed in such circumstances, as that the practice of its common duties, after a full conviction of the truth of it, should require attention, solicitude, and pains; or why appearing doubtfulness should be permitted to afford matter of temptation to some; as why external difficulties and allurements should be permitted to afford matter of temptation to others. The same account also is to be given, why some should be exercised with temptations of both these kinds, as why others should be exercised with the latter in such very high degrees, as some have been, particularly as the primitive Christians were.

Nor does there appear any absurdity in supposing that the speculative difficulties in which the evidence of religion is involved, may make even the principal part of some persons' trial. For as the chief temptations of the generality of the world, are the ordinary motives to injustice or unrestrained pleasure; or to live in the neglect of religion, from that frame of mind, which renders many persons almost without feeling as to any thing distant, or which is not the object of their senses; so there are other persons without this shallowness of temper, persons of a deeper sense as to what is invisible and future, who not only see, but have a general practical feeling, that what is to come will be present, and that things are not less real, for their not being the objects of sense; and who, from their natural constitution of body and of temper, and from their external condition, may have small temptations to behave ill, small difficulty in behaving well, in the common course of life. Now when these latter persons any possible doubts or difficulties, the practice of it is to them unavoidable, unless they will do a constant violence to their own minds; and religion is scarce any more a discipline to them, than have a distinct, full conviction of the truth of religion, without it is to creatures in a state of perfection. Yet these persons may possibly stand in need of moral discipline and exercise in a higher degree than they would have by such an easy practice of religion. Or it may be requisite, for reasons unknown to us, that they should give some further manifestations what is their moral character, to the creation of God, than such a practice of it would be. Thus in the great variety of religious situations in which men are placed, what constitutes, what chiefly and peculiarly constitutes the probation, in all senses, of some persons, may be the difficulties in which the evidence of religion is involved; and their principal and distinguished trial may be, how they will behave under and with respect to these difficulties. Circumstances in men's situation in their temporal capacity, analogous in good measure to this, respecting religion, are to be observed. We find some persons are placed in such a situation in the world, as that their chief difficulty, with regard to conduct, is not the doing what is prudent when it is known; for this, in numberless cases, is as easy as the contrary: but to some, the principal exercise is, recollection, and being upon their guard against deceits, the deceits suppose of those about them; against false appearances of reason and prudence. To persons in some situations, the principal exercise, with respect to conduct, is attention, in order to inform themselves what is proper, what is really the reasonable and prudent part to act.

But as I have hitherto gone upon *supposition, that men's dissatisfaction with the evidence of religion, is not owing to their neglects or prejudices;* it must be added, on the other hand, in all common reason, and as what the truth of the case plainly requires should be added, *that such dissatisfaction possibly may be owing to those, possibly may be men's own fault.* For,

If there are any persons who never set themselves heartily, and in earnest, to be informed in religion; if there are any, who secretly wish it may not prove true, and are less attentive to evidence than to difficulties, and more to objections, than to what is said in answer to them; these persons will scarce be thought in a likely way of seeing the evidence of religion, though it were most certainly true, and capable of being ever so fully proved. If any accustom themselves to consider this subject usually in the way of mirth and sport; if they attend to forms and representations, and inadequate manners of expression, instead of the real things intended by them, (for signs often can be more than inadequately expressive of the things signified); or if they substitute human errors in the room of divine truth; why may not all, or any of these things, hinder some men from seeing that evidence, which really is seen by others; as a like turn of mind, with respect to matters of common speculation and practice, does, we find by experience, hinder them from attaining that knowledge and right understanding, in matters of common specu- lation and practice, which more fair and attentive minds attain to? And the effect will be the same, whether their neglect of seriously considering the evidence of religion, and their indirect behavior with regard to it, proceed from mere carelessness or from the grosser vices; or whether it be owing to this, that forms, and figurative manners of expression, as well as errors, administer occasions of ridicule, when the things intended, and the truth it- self, would not. Men may indulge a ludicrous turn so far, as to lose all sense of conduct and prudence in worldly affairs, and even as it seems, to impair their faculty of reason. And in general, levity, carelessness, passion, and prejudice, do hinder us from be- ing rightly informed with respect to common things; and they may, in like manner, and perhaps in some farther providential manner, with respect to moral and religious subjects; may hinder evidence from being laid before us, and from being seen when it is. The Scripture does declare, that every one shall not under- stand.[1] And it makes no difference by what providential conduct this come to pass; whether the evidence of Christianity was, orig- inally and with design, put and left so, as that those who are desirous of evading moral obligations, should not see it, and that honest-minded persons should; or whether it comes to pass by any other means.

Farther: the general proof of natural religion and of Christianity, does, I think, lie level to common men: even those, the greatest part of whose time, from childhood to old age, is taken up with providing, for themselves and their families, the common conveniences, perhaps necessaries, of life; those, I mean, of this rank, who ever think at all of asking after proof, or attending to it. Common men, were they as much in earnest about religion as about their temporal affairs, are capable of being convinced upon real evidence, that there is a God who governs the world; and they feel themselves to be of a moral nature, and accountable creatures. And as Christianity entirely falls in with this their natural sense of things, so they are capable, not only of being persuaded, but of being made to see, that there is evidence of miracles wrought in attestation of it, and many appearing completions of prophecy. But though this proof is real and conclusive yet it is liable to objections, and may be run up into difficulties; which, however, persons who are capable, not only of talking of, but of really seeing, are capable also of seeing through; i. e. not of clearing up and answering them, so as to satisfy their curiosity, for of such knowledge we are not capable with respect to any one thing in nature; but capable of seeing that the proof is not lost in these difficulties, or destroyed by these objections. But then a thorough examination into religion, with regard to these objections, which cannot be the business of every man, is a matter of pretty large compass, and from the nature of it, requires some knowledge, as well as time and attention, to see how the evidence comes out, upon balancing one thing with another, and what, upon the whole, is the amount of it. Now if persons who have picked up these objections from others, and take for granted they are of weight, upon the word of those from whom they received them, or by often retailing of them, come to see, or fancy they see, them to be of weight, will not prepare themselves for such an examination, with a competent degree of knowledge; or will not give that time and attention to the subject, which, from the nature of it, is necessary for attaining such information: in this case, they must remain in doubtfulness, ignorance, or error; in the same way as they must with regard to common sciences, and matters of common life, if they neglect the necessary means of being informed in them.

But still perhaps it will be objected, that if a prince or common master were to send directions to a servant, he would take care that they should always bear the certain marks who they came from, and that their sense should be always plain; so as that there should be no possible doubt, if he could help it, concerning the authority or meaning of them. Now the proper answer to all this kind of objections is, that wherever the fallacy lies, it is even certain we cannot argue thus with respect to him who is the governor of the world; and particularly, that he does not afford us such information, with respect to our temporal affairs and interests, as experience abundantly shows. However, there is a full answer to this objection, from the very nature of religion. For, the reason why a prince would give his directions in this plain manner is, that he absolutely desires such an external action should be done, without concerning himself with the motive or principle upon which it is done; i. e. he regards only the external event, or the things' being done, and not at all, properly speaking, the doing of it, or the action. Whereas, the whole of morality and religion consisting merely in action itself, there is no sort of parallel between the cases. But if the prince be supposed to regard only the action; i. e. only to desire to exercise, or in any sense prove, the understanding or loyalty of a servant, he would not always give his orders in such a plain manner. It may be proper to add, that the will of God, respecting morality and religion, may be considered, either as absolute, or as only conditional. If it be absolute, it can only be thus, that we should act virtuously in such given circumstances; not that we should be brought to act so, by his changing of our circumstances. And if God's will be thus absolute, then it is in our power, in the highest and strictest sense, to do or to contradict his will; which is a most weighty consideration. Or his will may be considered only as conditional,—that if we act so and so, we shall be rewarded; if otherwise, punished: of which conditional will of the Author

of Nature, the whole constitution of it affords most certain instances.

Upon the whole: that we are in a state of religion necessarily
implies, that we are in a state of probation: and the credibility of
our being at all in such a state being admitted, there seems no
peculiar difficulty in supposing our probation to be, just as it is,
in those respects which are above objected against. There seems
no pretense, from the reason of the thing, to say, that the trial
cannot equitably be any thing, but whether persons will act suit-
ably to certain information, or such as admits no room for doubt;
so as that there can be no danger of miscarriage, but either from
their not attending to what they certainly know, or from overbearing passion hurrying them on to act contrary to it. For, since
ignorance and doubt afford scope for probation in all senses, as
really as intuitive conviction or certainty; and since the two former are to be put to the same account, as difficulties in practice;
men's moral probation may also be, whether they will take due
care to inform themselves by impartial consideration, and afterwards whether they will act as the case requires, upon the evidence which they have, however doubtful. And this, we find by
experience, is frequently our probation, in our temporal capacity.
For the information which we want, with regard to our worldly
interests, is by no means always given us of course, without any
care of our own. And we are greatly liable to self-deceit from
inward secret prejudices; and also to the deceit of others. So that
to be able to judge what is the prudent part, often requires much
and difficult consideration. Then after we have judged the very
best we can, the evidence upon which we must act, if we will
live and act at all, is perpetually doubtful to a very high degree.
And the constitution and course of the world in fact is such, as
that want to impartial consideration what we have to do, and
venturing upon extravagant courses, because it is doubtful what
will be the consequences are often naturally, i. e. providentially,
altogether as fatal, as misconduct occasioned by heedless inattention to what we certainly know, or disregarding it from overbearing passion.

Several of the observations here made may well seem strange, perhaps unintelligible to many good men. But if the persons for whose sake they are made, think so; persons who object as above, and throw off all regard to religion under pretense of want of evidence; I desire them to consider again, whether their think-ing so, be owing to any thing unintelligible in these observations, or to their own not having such a sense of religion, and serious solicitude about it, as even their state of scepticism does in all reason require? It ought to be forced upon the reflection of these persons, that our nature and condition necessarily require us, in the daily course of life, to act upon evidence much lower than what is commonly called probable; to guard not only against what we fully believe will, but also against what we think it supposable may, happen; and to engage in pursuits when the probability is greatly against success, if it be credible that possibly we may succeed in them.

[1]Dan. xii. 10. See also Isaiah xxix. 13, 14. Matt. vi. 23, and xi. 25, and xiii.11,12. John iii.19, and v.44. 1 Cor. ii.14, and 2 Cor. iv.4. 2 Tim.iii.13, and that affectionate, as well as authoritative admonition, so very many times inculcated, "He that hath ears to hear, let him hear." Grotius saw so strongly the thing intended in these and other passages of Scripture of the like sense, as to say, that the proof given us of Christianity was less than it might have been, for this very purpose: Ut ita sermo Evangelii tanquam lapis esset Lydius ad quem ingenia sanabilia explorarentur. De Ver. R.C. lib.2, toward the end. (We give the passage from Grotius in full: "If there be any one who is not satisfied with the arguments hitherto alleged for the truth of the Chris-tian religion, but desires more powerful ones, he ought to know that different things must have different kinds of proof; one sort in mathe-matics, another in the properties of bodies, another in doubtful mat-ters, and another in matters of fact. And we are to abide by that whose testimonies are void of all suspicion: if this be not admitted, not only all history is of no further use, and a great part of physic; but all that natural affection, which is between parents and children, is lost, who can be known no other way. And it is the will of God, that those things which he would have us believe, so as that faith should be accepted from us as obedience, should not be so very plain, as those things we perceive by onr senses, and by demonstration; but only so far as is sufficient to procure the belief, and persuade a man of the thing, who is not obstinately bent against it: So that the gospel is, as it were, a touchstone, to try men's honest dispositions by."